PRAISE FOR TARRA MISSIO
THE FAMILY COMPANION

A captivating adventure traversing many worlds, engaging readers in lessons of responsibility, courage, cooperation, kindness, forgiveness, and generosity- the many expressions of universal love. The protagonists' rich vocabularies expand the book reader's idea of what it means to be human and their place in the larger collective and planetary galactic whole. The Family Companion offers further educational content, many fun activities and suggestions for families and groups to enjoy together, encouraging the building of exploratory and observatory skills that are infused with higher-level aspirations, fortifying inner resources of intuition and imagination.

Celine Lim
Cht. Life Coach
Canada

TARRA Mission to Earth The Family Companion

Copyright © 2022 by Inna Van Der Velden

TARRA Mission To Earth
The Family Companion

All rights reserved.
No part of this work may be used or reproduced, transmitted, stored or used in any form or by any means graphic, electronic, or mechanical, including but not limited to photocopying, recording, scanning, digitizing, taping, Web distribution, information networks or information storage and retrieval systems, or in any manner whatsoever without prior written permission from the publisher.

This book contains works of fiction. Names, characters, places, and incidents either are the product of the author's imagination or are used fictitiously, and any resemblance to actual persons, living or dead, business establishments, events, or locales is entirely coincidental.

Disclaimer: The information provided in this book is strictly for informational purposes and is not intended as a substitute for advice from your physician or mental health provider. You should not use this information for diagnosis or treatment of any mental health problem.

Cover Art by Jaroslava Tretiakova

Publisher: Inna Van Der Velden
<Address>

ISBN: (Paperback) 978-1-7782551-1-3

Books may be purchased for educational, business, or sales promotional use.
For bulk order requests and price schedule contact:
5elementsrejuvenation@gmail.com

To dearest Patty and Peter with love,
Inna

TARRA
Mission to Earth
The Family Companion

By Inna Van Der Velden

Contents

Introduction: 1

Task 1

    Master Live Breathing 2

    Master Live Breathing: Adult Guide 6

Task 2

    Speak Vocal Tarrian 10

    Speak Vocal Tarrian: Adult Guide 12

Task 3

    I See You, You See Me 16

    I See You, You See Me: Adult Guide 18

Task 4

    Be the Leopard 20

    Be the Leopard: Adult Guide 22

Task 5

    Meet Your Shadow Animal 24

    Meet Your Shadow Animal: Adult Guide... 26

Task 6

    Play with Water 30

    Play with Water: Adult Guide 32

Task 7

    Eat like a Tarrian 34

    Eat like a Tarrian: Adult Guide 38

Task 8

    Experience Living Wind 42

    Experience Living Wind: Adult Guide 44

Task 9

    Tame the Angry Wind 46

    Tame the Angry Wind: Adult Guide 48

Task 10

    Speak to a Tree... 50

    Speak to a Tree: Adult Guide.. 52

Task 11

    Share Love with Earth... 54

    Share Love with Earth: Adult Guide 56

Task 12

    Plant a Friendship Tree 58

    Plant a Friendship Tree: Adult Guide 60

Task 13

    Create Live Water.. 62

    Create Live Water: Adult Guide... 64

Task 14

    Clean Your Place of Joy.. 66

    Clean Your Place of Joy: Adult Guide... 68

Task 15

    Dance in Gratitude.. 70

    Dance in Gratitude: Adult Guide... 72

Task 16

    Tell a Joke 74

    Tell a Joke: Adult Guide 76

Task 17

    Share a Joyful Experience 78

    Share a Joyful Experience: Adult Guide 80

Task 18

    Reconcile Relationships... 82

    Reconcile Relationships: Adult Guide 84

Task 19
- Draw a Dream..86
- Draw a Dream: Adult Guide...88

Task 20
- The Shadow Animals' School 90
- The Shadow Animal Class: Adult Guide 102

Task 21
- Create Shadow Animals Wisdom Cards...106
- Create Animal Wisdom Cards: Adult Guide...................................108

Task 22
- Draw a Birdhouse..110
- Draw a Birdhouse: Adult Guide..112

Task 23
- Learn a Lesson..114
- Learn a Lesson: Adult Guide..116

Task 24
- The Fire Shower..118
- The Fire Shower: Adult Guide..120

Task 25
- Experience a Foreign Word 124
- Experience a Foreign Word: Adult Guide 126

Task 26
- Make a Snowflake 128
- Make a Snowflake: Adult Guide 130

Task 27
- Make a Wish for our Earth..132
- Make a Wish for our Earth: Adult Guide..134

Task 28
- Walk Your Future 136
- Walk Your Future: Adult Guide 138

Task 29
- Conquer Your Fear 140
- Conquer Your Fear: Adult Guide 142

Task 30
- The Other Side of Fear 144
- The Other Side of Fear: Adult Guide 146

Task 31
- Feel Brave 148
- Feel Brave: Adult Guide 150

Task 32
- What is Ara? 152
- What is Ara?: Adult Guide 154

Task 33
- Draw Tarra 156
- Draw Tarra: Adult Guide 158

Task 34
- Tarrian Five Elements Radiance Drink 160
- Tarrian Five Elements Radiance Drink: Adult Guide 162

A Family Companion 164
- Further Reading: 164

v

INTRODUCTION:

Dear Readers,

The Tarrian mission urgently needs your help!

Together with our friends: Anthony, Lissy, Andy, the Saashes, and Audrey, you will have to perform thirty-four tasks to help them complete the mission. On the way, you will develop a lot of extraordinary Tarrian skills and will become as cool as Tarrians.

The book is designed as a family companion to *TARRA: Mission to Earth* for children and their parents/supervising adults. Each task has two parts: one for a child to complete and one as a guide for an adult to explore, contemplate, and help the child complete the task.

The part for children opens deeper awareness of the self, their dormant extraordinary abilities, the Earth, and the elements of nature. It explores the hidden potentials of the mind and takes a few steps into the unknown and magical. Children will accompany their favorite characters all the way from the beginning of their adventure to the glorious completion of the mission.

The part for adults explains the tasks and the ideas, concepts, and science which stand behind them. It also suggests more topics for exploration and in-depth discussions with your child along with resources in the back for further reading.

Some of the tasks are recorded so that the energy can be felt and experienced. They are found on the website: www.5elementsrejuvenation.com

We invite the whole family to participate, explore, and have fun!

Bon voyage!

TASK 1
Master Live Breathing

From Chapter 2, The Journey and the Singing Meadow:

When Anthony landed in the Rocky Mountains of Canada, he found out that the breaking wave separated him from his friends. He started panicking. His breathing became shallow, and he was about to faint. At this point, Anthony was still new on Earth and his body hadn't got used to completely different life patterns of this planet, including breathing. However, Anthony took charge and commanded himself "Stop and do live breathing!"

Do you remember how Tarrians breathe?

On Tarra, children learn to be aware of how they breathe. This process was called *live breathing*. The first thing children did when they woke up in the morning was take a few deep breaths in and out. While they were breathing, they were observing their breaths and their bodies. Then something miraculous would happen. They would merge with it, becoming one with their own breathing.

Dear Readers,

This is your first task in helping the mission! Let us all breathe together and help Anthony calm down and adjust to the breathing rhythm of our Earth with the help of live breathing. Mastering live breathing is your first step to become a true Tarrian.

Stop everything you are doing, sit comfortably and concentrate on breathing into your belly. When you breathe in and out, the air makes the diaphragm, which is the muscle above your stomach, expand and contract. You will feel how your tummy becomes bigger with each inhalation and smaller with each exhalation. As we count, breathe deeper and deeper.

Put one hand on your upper chest and the other just below your ribs.

Breathe in slowly through your nose so that your belly moves out against your hand. For the most effective breath, the hand on your chest will move very little, or not at all. If it does, no problem; you'll get better with practice. The focus is on bringing the breath down into the belly.

In your mind, keep the connection between your two hands and think only about your breath, nothing else.

Now start breathing. If a thought comes into your head, let it pass. If you feel you need to say something, try not to. Concentrate only on your breath.

Breathe in and out for a count of two. One, two..., and out... one, two...

Breathe in...one, two..., and out... one, two.

Now let's breathe more deeply. Breathe in... one, two, three, four, and out... one, two, three four... And again...

Now, let's go even deeper: breathe in... one, two, three, four, five, six, and breathe out... one, two, three four, five, six... And do it again... Your attention is only on your breath... Only your breath matters...

Take your time... Breathe for a minute or more until you become calm, and your breath has deepened.

Let Anthony catch up with you... Breathe in... one, two, three, four, five, six... and out... one, two, three, four, five, six...

Breathe in... one, two, three, four, five, six... and out... one, two, three, four, five, six... and soften... imagine your body getting softer and heavier...

Feel that every cell of your body and your breath are connected. Imagine that you can breathe through each cell of your body and all of them at the same time. Keep on breathing to the count of six.

Now, imagine that your breath merges with the breath of our planet Earth. Breathe together, Earth and you, and observe what is happening…

Connect more and more with your breath. It has merged with every cell of your body and with Earth at the same time. There is no separation. You have expanded and become one big breath! This type of breathing is called "live breathing" on Tarra.

How did live breathing help Anthony?

What was your experience of live breathing through every cell of your body and together with Earth?

What do you understand live breathing to be?

TASK 1
Master Live Breathing: Adult Guide

Topics to explore:

1. A scientific perspective on breathing
2. The difference between deep (calm) and shallow (rapid) breathing
3. Releasing stress, anger, and resentments with deep, mindful breathing
4. Being in the moment
5. Awareness of the breathing cycle of a person and the rhythm of life
6. Anthony's skill of live breathing

1. A scientific perspective on breathing

When we inhale air (which contains the most critical element to us, oxygen), it goes into our lungs. Our brain sends a message to the diaphragm, the muscle under our lungs, to move downwards. It allows the air to come into the body. The lungs extract the oxygen from the air. It is then absorbed into the red blood cells. The oxygen is transported via our blood to our organs and tissues. The waste product, carbon dioxide, is eliminated from the body when we breathe out.

2. The difference between deep (calm) and shallow (rapid) breathing

Shallow, rapid breathing draws minimal oxygen into the lungs, while deep, calm breathing into the stomach allows the body to obtain maximum oxygen. Most people are not aware of their breathing pattern during the day. If their breathing is shallow as often happens when people are stressed or anxious, they are not getting maximum oxygen into their system. This means that their organs are not going to be able to operate as well as they could and should. In a worst-case scenario, a person may even fight for breath, which is very scary. On the other hand, when people are relaxed, they normally breathe more deeply. When we become aware of deep breathing, we teach our mind and our body the best pattern for life.

3. **Releasing stress, anger, and resentments with deep, mindful breathing**

   When we are angry, stressed, anxious, or resentful, the whole body changes its calm and healthy "thriving" patterns and reorganizes its internal resources to cope with stress. These emergency measures require extra energy resources. One of the body's self-coping mechanisms is shallow breathing. A stressed person takes shallow, small breaths using the shoulders rather than the diaphragm to move the air. This is the pattern the body uses in an emergency. However, it is energy consuming. It also disrupts the normal gas exchange in the lungs which can lead to potential health issues.

   An alternative and healthier way to cope with stress is to be prepared for it by teaching your body a deep breathing pattern. Then, when a stressful situation occurs, you are in control. You are aware of what is happening. You know how to overthrow this energy consuming pattern and to bring your body back to a healthy state, which is deep, relaxed breathing.

4. **Being in the moment**

   While doing this task, encourage children to close their eyes and focus on breathing. If a thought comes, let it pass by. Being in the moment of life is very important. This is the moment when we don't have to think about the past or worry about the future. We can choose to be happy now. Being in the moment creates happiness and health.

5. **Awareness of the breathing cycle of a person and the rhythm of life**

   When we breathe in and out, we connect not only with the rhythm of breathing in our body but also with the rhythm of life itself. Giving and receiving, active movement and periods of resting, changes of day and night, the change of seasons, the waxing and waning moon, and the tidal movements are all parts of this rhythm. You may want to introduce the concept of the rhythm of life to children and ask them to give you other examples. Encourage the children to share their experience of imagining merging their breath with the breath of Earth. It is unique and precious. It gives them a bigger awareness that they, too, are part of life on Earth.

6. **Anthony's skill of live breathing**

In the book, Anthony employed the skill of live breathing like it is done on Tarra. In our understanding, live breathing is a combination of mindful, deep breathing and a bigger awareness of the mutual breath of your whole body and Earth. Live breathing helped Anthony to better adjust to his life on Earth in several ways. First, it allowed him to calm down and to prevent hyperventilation and fainting in an emergency situation. Secondly, he was able to better connect to his Earth body, its energies, and all of its cells. Finally, Anthony was able to expand his breath and merge with the flow of Earth breathing. He no longer felt separate from the new planet, or that he "did not belong" there. On the contrary, he acquired a sense of deep connection and being in the flow with Earth's life.

TASK 2
Speak Vocal Tarrian

Dear Readers,

Do you remember from Chapter 2 that our friends communicate in silent Tarrian as well as in vocal Tarrian? Vocal Tarrian is all about having fun with rhyming.

Would you like to try speaking vocal Tarrian as well?

Combine the following three sentences into a rhymed phrase.
Feel free to move the words wherever you need to get something snappy. You don't have to use every word.

When you are completely happy with your result, it means that you have completed the second task.

>   The moon juice is calming and cooling.
>   It helps me sleep peacefully.
>   I am going to drink a cup of the moon juice before I go to bed.

Write down your own rhymed phrase below:

Come up with and write down your own three sentences for your friend to rhyme. These three sentences should reflect Tarra's life the way you imagine it.

What facts do you remember about the Tarrian language?

TASK 2
Speak Vocal Tarrian: Adult Guide

Topics to explore:

1. The Tarrian language
2. The challenges of rhyming
3. Extracting the main idea from the three sentences and producing a rhyme
4. Having fun
5. Advantages of cooperation
6. Multiple ways to solve the same problem
7. Possible discussions

1. The Tarrian language

The Universal Tarrian language is the global language for communication on Tarra. There are two varieties of the Tarrian language: silent and vocal.

Silent Tarrian involves communication in a telepathic mode, in images, concepts (like bravery or kindness), and direct thoughts. Draw the children's attention to the fact that Tarrians' minds can receive and process several images, concepts, or thoughts at the same time.

Encourage children to answer the following questions:
Which variety of Tarrian is a more efficient for communication, silent or vocal?
Which variety is more fun?
Which variety would be more appropriate in the following situations: emergency, party, solving a problem, speaking to a friend, etc.?
In Task 2, a child will get a taste of how to speak vocal Tarrian.

2. The challenges of rhyming

Rhyming has its challenges.
Start with recognizing the rhyme.
Be aware of easy and difficult words to rhyme.
Encourage a child to rhyme some simple words first and then try a few more challenging words, where perhaps the rhyme only happens in the last syllable.

Simple words: moon-soon, juice-moose, sleep-deep.
Difficult words: peaceful-beautiful, graceful-useful, emergency-urgency etc.

3. Extracting the main idea from the three sentences and producing a rhyme

Teach children to underline the most important words in each sentence. For example:

The **moon juice** is **calming and cooling.**
It helps me **sleep** peacefully.
I am going to **drink** a cup of the moon juice before I go to bed.

Discuss the main idea(s) with them.

Write one sentence which incorporates the main idea, for example: "Drinking cooling moon juice helps me sleep." There can be several variations. Be open to all.

Encourage a child to produce a rhymed phrase, for example: "Adding moon to healthy drinks helps me catch my forty winks."

4. Having fun

One of the most important aspects of rhyming is to have fun! Vocal Tarrian is about having fun with rhyming words.

5. Advantages of cooperation

Let children work either individually or in groups. Discuss why cooperation makes a challenging task easier.

6. Multiple ways to solve the same problem

The same problem can be solved in multiple ways. Draw children's attention to this idea. How does it work in the adult world? Give examples.

7. Possible discussions

One topic for discussion is a possibility of a common language on Earth. You can give an example of creating the most well-known international language, Esperanto.

Esperanto was created in the 19th century by a Polish linguist, Dr. Zamenhov. He called it international language or neutral language. Esperanto has Latin roots, but the vocabulary comes from English, German, Polish, and Russian. Esperanto doesn't belong to any country in particular but people from 115 countries speak it. Twenty-five thousand books are written or translated into Esperanto, and some people speak it, among them are Pope John Paul II, the former UN translator Claude Piron, and former Austrian presidents, Franz Jonas and Heinz Fischer.

Another possible topic for discussion is telepathic communication between people. What might happen if people learn to read each other's thoughts? For one, a lie would be immediately apparent: one would have to speak the truth all the time, like on Tarra! On the other hand, when everyone's thoughts are clear, there is no miscommunication and no misunderstandings.

TASK 3
I See You, You See Me

Dear Readers,

The singing meadow told Anthony in Chapter 3, The Apple Frequency, "Find the purity of one, it will lead you to everyone."

When Anthony found a Master tree in Ben and Margo's garden, he was able to get in touch with his friends through the frequency of purity of the apple. Would you like to experience the frequency of purity yourself?

For that, you will need to choose a piece of fruit, like an apple or a banana, and tune into its vibration of purity. You readers live in many places on this Earth, even on different continents. When we do this exercise altogether, Anthony will feel flickers of purity everywhere. The signals will merge and become strong enough to cover the whole Earth. Then, he will finally be able to get in touch with his friends. Let us help him make it happen.

Take a piece of fruit in your hands. Notice everything about it: the temperature, the texture, the flow of the fruit juices, or something else.

Close your eyes and concentrate on feeling everything you can feel about it.

Say, "I touch you, and you touch me." When you are touching the fruit, feel its energies becoming part of yours, and yours becoming part of the fruit. Notice that what you are holding is alive.

When you have enjoyed this new sensation long enough, say, "I see you, and you see me." Open your eyes, see the fruit, and observe it for a while. Then close your eyes and start "seeing" it with your eyes closed. Feel its beautiful energy.

Say, "I smell you, and you smell me." Allow its smell to reach your smell buds, let it become part of you.

"I sense you, and you sense me." Appreciate what it feels likes to be this fruit and be open to what it might share with you. Notice everything you sense.

"I respect you, and you respect me." Let the appreciation of the fruit's existence on this Earth touch your heart. Send gratitude to it for being your food and supporting your life.

Now merge completely with the energies of the fruit and start feeling the frequency of purity of the fruit and say, "I am as pure as you are."

Share what the frequency of purity of the fruit felt like.

What did the fruit smell like?

What did you learn from touching it?

What did you "see" with your eyes closed?

What did you sense about it?

TASK 3
I See You, You See Me: Adult Guide

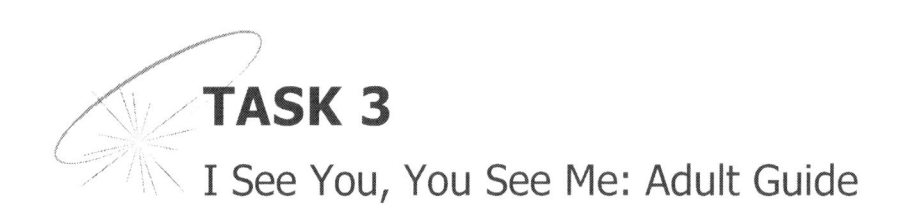

Topics to explore:

1. Awareness of our senses
2. Opening the senses of perception to the exploration of the fruit with awareness
3. Imagination and awareness

1. Awareness of our senses

People have five basic senses through which perception happens: touching, hearing, seeing, smelling, and tasting. Each sensing organ sends the information to the brain to perceive and process the environment around us.

In this task we engage touching, internal seeing, smelling, and sensing. In addition, you can include hearing and tasting if you want to encourage a child to explore all five basic senses.

Touch is the first sense a human develops. Through touch you get information about temperature, pressure, vibration, love, etc. Discuss the healing effect of a compassionate touch.

Seeing is a complex process. Light reflects off the object to the eye. Then the information is sent to the brain though the optic nerve as electrical impulses. In this task, you go beyond seeing with your eyes to "seeing" with your eyes closed. This is awareness about an object in space, which the brain forms without seeing the object with the actual eyes. Encourage your child to open up to the idea of awareness.

Smelling is another sense. The olfactory cleft on the roof of the nasal cavity transmits smells to the brain through the nerve ending. Humans have five million scent receptors in the nose, while dogs have one hundred million scent receptors.

Hearing involves a sound wave traveling through the external ear to the auditory canal and the eardrum into the middle ear. The sound wave is subsequently translated into electrical impulses and goes to the brain.

Through tasting, we perceive five basic tastes: sweet, salty, sour, bitter, and pungent (savory), according to Chinese philosophy. Humans perceive taste via their 2,000 and more taste buds. Most taste buds are located on the tongue, but some are in the throat and in the nasal cavity.

The sixth sense of perception explored in Task 3 might be new to some people. Sensing is receiving information based on a deeper perception of reality, without being able to explain how we get this information. We just know. Sensing is based on the feedback from engaging senses at a deeper level. For a Tarrian, it might be, for example, the journey a fruit makes from the moment the seed was planted into the soil until it is consumed. Encourage a child to experiment with sensing. Whatever information a child gets through sensing should be supported and praised.

2. **Opening the senses of perception to the exploration of the fruit with awareness**
   When we open the senses of perception to exploration, we go beyond regular seeing, touching, smelling, tasting, and hearing. In order to open yourself up, it is best to close your eyes. Encourage a child to describe what they have not noticed before about their senses and about the fruit when they explore it with awareness.

3. **Imagination and awareness**
   Some children will rely on their imagination. They will *imagine* the information about the fruit. However, other children will explore the fruit with *greater awareness* of it; they will engage internal knowing. Encourage a child to describe what they have noticed about the fruit they haven't known before.

TASK 4
Be the Leopard

Dear Readers,

Do you remember that Lissy couldn't summon her shadow leopard in Chapter 4, Meeting Shadow Animals? The team started helping her by creating the shadow leopard summoning signal, just the way they did it on Tarra.

> They saw yellowish fur and black spots all over their bodies. They could hear soft purring sounds coming from their mouths. They felt the need to hunt. They were leopards, dangerously wild and active one moment yet shy and lazy another. They heard themselves roaring, "I am my own being. I am my strength. My purpose is to survive." Each member of the group felt the qualities of the leopard streaming into their bodies. Their muscles were strengthening and acquiring incredible endurance. Their minds were empowered with perseverance.

Because the signal was not strong enough, they had to try even harder. At this time, the Tarrian team needs your assistance! Let's help Lissy summon her shadow animal.

Assume the pose of the animal and feel its strength in your own muscles. Just take your time to learn to be one. Imagine what it feels like to be a leopard. You already know what to do. Feel it, sense it, see it, speak it, and be it.

Share you experience. What does it feel like to be the leopard?

TASK 4
Be the Leopard: Adult Guide

Topics to explore:

1. The primal instincts in animals and humans
2. Awareness of your own muscles
3. Awareness of your energy levels

1. **The primal instincts in animals and humans**
   According to online dictionaries, primal instinct is the natural tendency of a person or an animal to behave or react in a particular way.

   Animals have primal instincts which help them survive, procreate, and cope with the dangers in their environment. They are, for example, protecting their young, hunting, mating, nest building, locating food, etc.

   Encourage children to be acquainted with the existence of primal instincts in humans and let them guess what some of these might be.

2. **Awareness of your own muscles**
   There are more than 600 muscles in your body. The muscles are made of elastic tissues like rubber. There are three types of muscles: smooth, cardiac, and skeletal. You can't control smooth muscles. For example, your stomach is made of smooth muscles. Indeed, you can't control digestion. It happens naturally. The cardiac muscles in your heart circulates blood around your body. You can't control this process either. The skeletal muscles help you run, exercise, swim, walk, etc. You can control them.

   Muscles make up forty percent of your body weight. Give examples of a few muscles. You flex your arm with the help of biceps. These muscles participate, for example, in lifting, pulling, and pushing. Quadriceps are located in your thighs. These muscles are very strong in athletes and runners.

3. Awareness of your energy levels

Help children be aware of personal energy levels. Discuss what gives energy to the body: fresh air, exercise, a healthy diet, rest, and positive emotions.

Fresh air is very important to supply the body with oxygen, thus invigorating the body.

Regular exercise builds up the strength of your muscles and makes your whole body stronger.

A healthy, balanced diet gives us the maximum amount of energy, vitamins, and minerals our bodies need to function to their best ability. Encourage children to learn more about healthy eating. One of the sources that gives simple but useful information is
https://www.webmd.com/parenting/guide/food-smart-kids#2

It is very important to alternate active time with rest time. By doing this, a person will not overexert themselves and will keep a healthy balance for their bodies to function at its healthiest level.

Discuss how our emotions affect our energy levels. Sadness, grief, or a bad mood lower our energy levels and make us tired. Ask children what they noticed about the energy levels of people who are grieving, sad, or in a bad mood.

On the other hand, discuss how happiness, joyful activities, and friendships raise the energy of the body. Notice how fun activities or creative projects make us happy and give us more energy.

Motivate the children to mark their energy levels on the scale of zero (the worst) to ten (the best). Help them understand the factors which might have influenced their energy levels: fresh air, exercise, diet, rest, and emotions.

TASK 5
Meet Your Shadow Animal

Dear Readers,

Just like Tarrians in Chapter 4, you can also meet your own shadow animal and be friends with them.

It is important you start with live breathing in order to slow down your thoughts and open up your senses. Do you remember how we did it? No rush, let us do it gradually.

Take your time...

Now imagine that Earth is going to give you a wonderful gift: the support of your very own shadow animal. Of course, it might also be a shadow bird, or a shadow marine creature, like a dolphin or a whale.

It is for you to discover and enjoy.

No rush, no need to try hard... Just close your eyes, focus on your breath, and wait for it to show up... Some of you might meet your shadow friend right away. Others might find it useful to prepare for the experience by mastering your deep breathing technique first. You will need to have a very quiet mind to allow this gift to become your treasure.

Dream, imagine, just be, and have a great experience!

Draw a picture of a shadow animal you have seen.

What kind of shadow animal did you get?

When you have mastered the skill of seeing your shadow animal, you can ask it a question. Start with a simple question, for example "What is your name?"

TASK 5
Meet Your Shadow Animal: Adult Guide

Topics to explore:

1. Scientific perspective on the brain functions
2. Two kinds of knowing: logical and intuitive versus direct
3. Meeting a shadow animal

   1. Scientific perspective on the brain functions
   When we talk about our brain, we really mean two halves, one on each side of the head. Each side, or hemisphere, controls the opposite side of the body. The left brain controls the right side of the body and is responsible for logic. The right brain controls the left side of the body and is responsible for intuition and imagination.

   In the modern world, most people's left brain is more developed. Such people are more logical and are good at exact sciences, like math. The left-brained people (or left dominant) typically use their right hand for writing.

   People with the dominant right brain more often use their left hand for writing and are more artistic and intuitive.

   However, some people use both hands equally well. It means that their left and right brains are quite balanced. Such people are good at both exact science and at artistic activities.

   Some of the functions of the brain are:
   - To form logical perceptions from the information coming from the world around us
   - To have intuitive ideas
   - To form memories from previous experiences
   - To have insights through deep intuitive understanding

- To dream (night dreaming and daydreaming)
- To know directly. The information is just there. ("I just know, I don't know how.")

2. **Two kinds of knowing: logical and intuitive versus direct**
   Direct knowing might be a new concept for many of us.

   Normally we get the information about ourselves, our planet, and the Universe through the more widely studied logical-intuitive process of our mind. The Mind activity is quite limited. It is the result of perceptions formed through seeing, hearing, touching, smelling, tasting, feeling, and thinking. The Mind wants to know about the Self through our senses.

   In this task, we explore the unknown function of our brain, which we call *direct knowing*. Direct knowing is the result of the state of being Self. Self KNOWS and IS at the same time.

   The information is already there, "we just know." It is easier for children than for adults to get access to direct knowing. Children's brains have not yet formed lots of beliefs about the world around them. The children's mind is more open to perceive information about Self and the Universe directly by BEING Self and JUST KNOWING.

3. **Meeting a shadow animal**
   The task of Meeting a Shadow Animal is an exploration into the unknown. It is about opening yourself to the magic of the Universe. It involves exploring a function of the Mind which is not yet fully understood, developed, or used.

   This activity is based on a combination of dreaming, imagination, and direct knowing. It depends on how a child's Mind will obtain the information.

   Note: Sometimes a shadow animal that a child may see reflects certain qualities of that child or complements his or her qualities.

Encourage sharing. It is fun and fascinating to observe what kind of shadow animals your child may encounter.

TASK 6
Play with Water

Dear Readers,

I am sure you loved the way Saash the boy and Water played together creating different tastes in Chapter 7. You probably look forward to your own experiment to see if works for you in the same way it worked for Saash. It is exciting to create magic together with the Water element! I am sure Saash would love to share his technique with you. Let us play with the Water element.

Pour a glass of Water. Sit down comfortably. Take the glass in both hands. Concentrate on your breathing. Deep, slow breathing is everything that matters. Breathe for a few minutes until your mind's chatter subsides. You feel only the movement of your breath in and out. Close your eyes.

Now bring your awareness to the Water in your glass. There is only Water; nothing else exists or matters. Feel its temperature, listen to its sound, imagine what it feels like to be pure water… Now imagine *being* Water. Spend a few minutes just being the Water in your glass.

Imagine Water is filled with something very sweet, like sugar or honey. Feel the love of Earth sharing its sweet taste with your water. Don't think about it, just feel it being sweet.

Now, taste the Water in your glass.

After your experiment, don't forget to bring the taste back to neutral. Just give it a command, "Back to neutral, please."

You can also experiment with other tastes. You can observe that Water tastes sour, bitter, or salty.

When you feel that you have mastered basic tastes, you can start adding flavors: peach, strawberry, mint, lemon, or maybe chocolate! Try them all and see which taste your Water will become.

It took the Saashes a long time to master this, so it might also take you a lot of practice to learn how to do this exercise. Do not rush, take your time. One day you will notice that you can do it. It will be your big magic!

Write down which taste you added to Water.

Describe what your Water tastes like.

Which flavor did you add to Water?

Describe what your Water tastes like.

TASK 6
Play with Water: Adult Guide

Topics to explore:

1. A scientific perspective on water
2. Five basic tastes
3. Developing abilities to communicate with Water

1. A scientific perspective on water

Water is a chemical liquid substance. Science says that water is the second most common molecule in the Universe.

Water covers seventy percent of Earth's surface. Oceans, lakes, seas, and rivers are made of water. The human body is seventy percent water. Our tissues, blood, body fluids, and even bones contain water. Children's bodies have more water than adults' bodies. When people age, water dissipates from the bodies; the bones become brittle, and the skin is less elastic. Neither people nor nature can live without water.

In 2004 a Japanese doctor, Masaru Emoto, wrote a book, *The Hidden Messages in Water,* which became a *New York Times* bestseller. In his book, Dr. Emoto stated that the molecular structure of water responded to and was transformed by exposure to people's words, thoughts, intentions, and sounds.

Loving words created symmetrical beautiful molecular forms, while angry or fearful words resulted in unpleasant, asymmetrical forms of the molecule.

Dr. Masaru Emoto took pictures of the water crystals created by both loving and non-loving words, thoughts, and music, which consistently reflected this.

Dr. Emoto's research also showed how polluted water can be remedied with loving thoughts, prayer, or exposure to beautiful music.

2. **Five basic tastes**

    According to Chinese medicine, our basic tastes are sweet, salty, sour, bitter, and pungent (savory). Our taste buds can identify the basic tastes as well as many other tastes and flavors. The sensory organs are located on the tongue, in the back of the throat, and on the roof of the mouth. People develop their sensory abilities gradually from their childhood, exposing their sensory organs to a variety of different tastes.

3. **Developing abilities to communicate with Water**

    Task 6 is about the exploration of our ability to communicate with the Water element.

    Because Water responds to our intention, thoughts, or words naturally, it is interesting to explore how the Water in your glass responds to you. You must encourage children to approach this experiment with loving thoughts and integrity. Remember it is just a game and an exploratory experiment.

TASK 7
Eat like a Tarrian

Dear Readers,

Do you remember from Chapter 7 how hard it was for Saash the boy to adjust his body to healthy eating on Earth?

> Baba Vera explained to Saash: "Your body's perception has changed on Earth. Your human senses are aligned with Earth energies, and your Tarrian senses are aligned with Tarrian energies. Now you need to figure out how to have them work together. You just have to learn to feel what is good for your body here."

Saash followed Baba Vera's advice. He applied his Tarrian perception of how to identify the best foods for his body to figure out which of Earth's foods are best for him.

Would you like to learn how to eat like a Tarrian? When you do, you might start noticing that you will naturally be attracted to healthier food and will grow to be a super strong and super healthy person, like a true Tarrian.

This task requires some preparation. First you need to be a little hungry to perform it. When you are, go to the kitchen and without much thinking choose five foods of five basic tastes (salty, sour, sweet, bitter, savory/pungent).

Write down what you have chosen:
    For salty-
    For sour-
    For sweet-
    For bitter-
    For savory (pungent)-
    Lay all five foods on the table in front of yourself.

Now, look at all five foods and ask your body which taste you are most attracted to: salty, sour, sweet, bitter, or savory (pungent). This will help you become aware of what taste your body craves. Note that food can be a combination of tastes (for example, an apple can be sweet and sour at the same time). Do not think about the particular food you have chosen, *feel* what taste your body is attracted to most at the moment.

An example. Let us say your body is attracted to salty chips you laid out on the table. Let us say it is a package of sea salt and malt vinegar chips.

You feel that you like it so much that you can eat the whole bag. Next, identify what other taste is present in the chips that your body is attracted to. Perhaps, it is also the sour taste.

You are aware that your body would like some food with salty and sour taste at this moment.

Now comes the *thinking* part. Do you think that you have chosen the healthiest food you have at home with the combination of salty and sour taste? If not, think about a healthier alternative. For a Tarrian, it would be food that is grown in nature and has the purest nature qualities. For a combination of salty and sour tastes, a true Tarrian would give preference to, for example, some dried seaweed (dulce) or half of an avocado sprinkled with sea salt and lemon rather than a bag of chips. They would do so because a true Tarrian appreciates high energy value to the body of foods that are grown in nature, more so than man-made foods, which typically contain chemical additives, taste amplifiers, etc.

Now, choose this healthy alternative, and eat it. You have supplemented your body with the taste it was craving but used a healthier alternative. After you have eaten, give your body ten to fifteen minutes to absorb the food. Now feel again whether your body is still attracted to a bag of chips, or if it is quite happy with what it already had.

Which basic taste or a combination of tastes was your body attracted to?

What food did you choose to supplement your craving for the taste with?

Was this food healthy and grown in nature?

If not, which healthier alternative did you choose in the end?

How do you feel after you have eaten a healthier alternative?

Was your friend attracted to the same taste?

Share your experience.

TASK 7
Eat like a Tarrian: Adult Guide

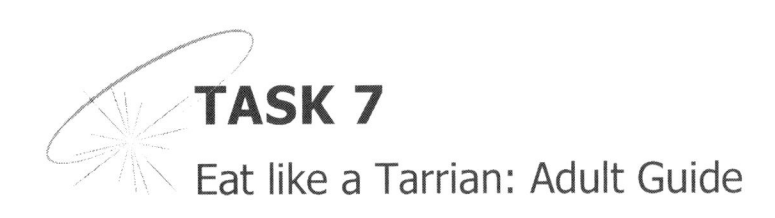

Topics to explore:

1. Five basic tastes from the perspective of Chinese medicine
2. Examples of healthy foods reflecting five basic tastes
3. What this task teaches your child
4. How to perform this task

1. Five basic tastes from the perspective of Chinese medicine

Chinese medicine states that all the food has five basic tastes or consists of a combination of five basic tastes.

From the Chinese medicine perspective, the five basic tastes also reflect the five basic elements of nature:
Salty taste reflects the Water element.
Sour taste reflects the Wood (Air) element.
Bitter (burnt) taste belongs to the Fire element.
Sweet taste is the attribute of the Earth element.
Savory (pungent) taste belongs to the Metal element.

2. Examples of healthy foods reflecting five basic tastes

Foods with salty tastes are the ones that have natural salt in them: dulce, kelp, fish, seaweed, or anything that comes from the sea.
The natural sour taste is in lemons, grapefruits, oranges, plums, sour apples, etc.

The bitter taste can be found in some herbs or vegetables: parsley, chicory, Belgium endives, celery, coffee, etc. It can also be something that is slightly burnt by the sun or the fire, for example, slightly burnt toast.

The sweet taste is the most popular in nature and is abundant in fruit, dry fruit, or root vegetables like carrots, potatoes, or yams. Every food that has some sweetness in it reflects the Earth element.

The savory (pungent) taste is found naturally in garlic, onion, turnips, parsnips, radishes, horseradish, etc. and is considered to reflect the energies of Metal.

3. **What this task teaches your child**

   This task teaches your child to listen to their bodies and identify what taste (flavor) their body is craving or attracted to. When you take time to listen to your body, you will have a better awareness of its needs. We often eat impulsively, because it is there, not because our body really needs it or gets the most energy value from the craving.

   When one has a better awareness of the body's needs, one will be able to better identify how to substitute some junk food with a healthier alternative, which has more energy value to the body.

   For example, dry raisins, dulce, lemon, berries of all kinds, etc. can be nutritious substitutes for candies, chips, and other unhealthy foods.

   This task also teaches a child a greater awareness of basic tastes or a combination of tastes in nature. A child will learn about themselves, and which tastes they are attracted to most.

   Children will be surprised to find out that their friends might be attracted to or have a craving for very different tastes than themselves which may also encourage more experimenting with foods.

4. **How to perform this task**

   We recognize that the easiest tastes for a child to experiment with will be salty, sour, and sweet. After your child manages to recognize a healthier alternative to these three basic tastes, you can introduce savory (pungent) and bitter tastes.

When your child performs the task for the first time, give minimal guidance to what food to choose for each taste. It will give both the child and you as a parent/supervising adult a chance to learn more about how your child eats and what unhealthy habits are already in place.

Encourage your child to always try a healthier alternative and start forming a healthier habit.

When the foods with three to five basic tastes are laid out on the table in front of the child, make sure that the child listens to their body before pointing to the food of their choice.

Make sure they choose the taste, and not a particular food.

TASK 8
Experience Living Wind

In Chapter 8, Lissy's "genius splash" is the ability to connect to Wind at a deeper level. Wind taught her to be fast, eager, experimental, friendly, and loving! Lissy taught Jakov the first step to a deeper connection with Wind.

Dear Readers,

Would you like to join Jakov in this experience? Lissy would love to teach you too!

Please, go outside. You might want to choose a slightly windy day for this exercise. Stand or sit in a quiet, open place, where you can feel the movement of the Wind. Relax your body and start breathing. You already know how to do this. As you breathe deeper and deeper, your mind's chatter will subside. Only your breathing matters, nothing else.

Close your eyes and start noticing Wind and its movement on your face, on your arms and legs. Nothing else matters anymore but your own breathing with Wind. In and out, in and out.

Allow your breath to connect to the breath of Wind, find a comfortable pattern of breathing together. Just be Wind which is breathing through you and with you. You have merged with Wind completely. At one moment you might notice that Wind is alive. It has its own patterns, its own life. Wind invites you to be its friend and experience its life. You have now become part of Living Wind. Breathe for a while... and just **be** Living Wind, notice things about it that you haven't noticed before. When you are ready, you can speak to it and ask Living Wind questions.

When you have enjoyed experiencing Living Wind enough, you can send your gratitude to it. Disconnect yourself from Wind in your mind and become yourself again.

What did you learn from being Living Wind?

What questions did you ask Living Wind?

What answers did you get back?

TASK 8
Experience Living Wind: Adult Guide

Topics to explore:

1. The scientific perspective on wind
2. The Chinese philosophical and medical perspectives on the five elements of nature, including Wind (Air)
3. Observing Wind on a deeper level and having fun

1. The scientific perspective on wind

Wind is the movement of air, created by the change in air pressure. Depending on its strengths, we use different names to describe wind: e.g., a breeze, a gale, a storm, a tornado, a hurricane, etc. The energy of the wind is harnessed and used by people to create electricity. Wind turbines are used in some countries (the Netherlands and Denmark) to generate up to twenty percent of the total electrical production replacing old-fashioned windmills and polluting power plants.

2. The Chinese philosophical and medical perspectives on the five elements of nature, including Wind (Air)

According to Chinese philosophy and medicine, two huge types of consciousness exist in the Universe: yin and yang. Yin corresponds to the female energy, night, rest, coolness, and nurturing. Yang reflects the male energy, day, action, warmth, and exploration.

The interplay of these two big forces created the five elements of nature: Water, Air, Fire, Earth, and Metal. They are considered smaller, yet still big types of consciousness. It is believed that everything we see on this Earth was born out of these five elements.

Air (Wind) itself is a child-like element, a young spirit. It is characterized by fast movements in different directions and lots of child energy and vitality. The positive quality of Wind is curiosity. The negative quality of Wind is considered anger and frustration. In the book, Lissy expresses the full array of Wind qualities: fast moving, curious, and full of beaming energy, as well as the tendency to get easily frustrated and angry.

3. **Observing Wind on a deeper level and having fun**
   The objective of this task is to have a closer encounter with the Wind element, to notice its qualities, and to have fun. This task is all about observation and deeper connection with the element. The results children may get are not as important as their deeper awareness of this element.

   Note: The task is called Experience Living Wind because Tarrians believe that Wind has consciousness and is alive.

TASK 9
Tame the Angry Wind

Do you remember how Lissy was taming the angry Wind, throwing around green feathers back in Chapter 1, Tarra and the Mission? She also showed the angry Wind within Lady Mieka to do the same so that she could calm down quickly.

> "I also get angry fast," admitted Jakov. "Can you teach the Wind within me to throw around green feathers, so that I will learn how to calm down?"
>
> "It's quite easy, Jakov," said Lissy and explained, "Every time you get angry, just imagine green feathers blowing out of your body. The angrier you are, the more feathers will come flying out. Don't think about the reason why you got angry. Focus only on watching the feathers. What you always want to do is to calm yourself down enough so that the feathers stop flying."
>
> "It sounds quite easy," said Jakov, surprised at how Lissy was taming Wind.
>
> "It is simple when you are calm. It is a different story when you are angry. That's why you have to practice it," said Lissy. "It is like you are teaching your dog obedience; it takes time and patience. So, it will take a few times before the angry Wind inside you remembers what to do."

Dear Readers!

I am sure you might want to join Jakov in this experience when you notice the angry Wind inside you. When you notice even the slight signs of angry Wind inside yourself, start swinging your arms and turning your neck while imagining bright green feathers coming out of your arms, mouth, and even nose! Have fun taming Wind!

Did you manage to tame the angry Wind when you encountered it?

What was the experience like?

TASK 9
Tame the Angry Wind: Adult Guide

Topics to explore:

1. Emotion anger from a scientific perspective
2. Lissy's way to overcome anger

1. Emotion anger from a scientific perspective

Anger is a natural response of a person to existing or perceived danger. However, it could be harmful for a person's health. In order to minimize harm to the body, we need to learn about anger and find a way to manage it. The root of anger is in the brain. When a provoking event occurs, our brain reacts by sending to our body a "fight or flight" response. The brain tells the body to release the hormones cortisol and adrenaline. The body responds to the flow of these hormones in a particular way:

- The heart rate increases so that more blood can be sent to your arms to fight and legs to run.
- Breathing becomes more rapid so that there is more oxygen coming into the lungs.
- The face becomes flushed.
- Muscles become tense and ready for a response, even the tummy becomes tense.
- There is no hunger as the body is prepared for the response.

This response of the body requires a lot of energy, that is why after angry episodes, it is necessary to restore the energy. Restful activities help, like walking in the woods or doing something soothing and positive.

2. Lissy's way to overcome anger

In the book, Lissy experiments with this negative emotion of Wind (anger) by throwing around green feathers.

Lissy's way to manage anger is to overcome this energy by not taking herself seriously. By recognizing that anger is an emotional energy, which has its patterns in the body, it becomes easier to treat it as such and to overcome it faster.

Note: There are two polarities to each emotion. Anger is the negative polarity at one end of a continuum, and calmness is a positive polarity at the other end. In life, we are always somewhere on this continuum. We may be close to one or the other polarity, or we may be somewhere in between. Awareness of this is a necessary pre-requisite to learning to recognize anger and manage it.

TASK 10
Speak to a Tree

Dear Readers,

From Chapter 10, we learn that Jakov is one of the people on our Earth who can speak to trees. This skill is extraordinary! Lissy was very keen to learn it from the Earth boy. She looked forward to hearing Opa Oak's voice and to getting some clues from him on how to help the mission.

Because you are also eager to help Anthony's mission, let us do this exercise together. Perhaps the tree you choose to speak to one day will share how Earth can fight pollution.

For this exercise it is best to go outside and choose a tree you would like to speak with. It can be any tree, but the most important thing is to be drawn to it intuitively, with your heart.

Sit comfortably on a bench or right on the grass. Close your eyes and start breathing. Let your breath become deeper and deeper. Wait till your mind is very quiet. Next, drop your attention to your heart. Feel as if a communication door opens within it. Now you are ready for a conversation with the tree.

Introduce yourself to the tree. Tell it how much you love it and appreciate its presence in your life. Spend a few moments just listening to the tree's leaves and branches swaying in the wind. Feel the strength of its trunk, the elasticity of its branches, and the reliability of its root system. Feel that the tree is ready to speak to you. If it is not, you will know!

In your mind, imagine that you are a light feather, which is gently falling from the skies. It dances around the sky, approaching the tree in soft swirls. As soon as you touch the tree, you are completely absorbed by it. You have become part of it.

Ask the tree a question like you ask a person, "What's your name?" "What are you doing here?"

Come and see the same tree a few times and always ask the tree the same question until you hear the voice of this tree.

When the tree gets used to your presence, you will become good friends. It will listen to you when you are in need, and it will answer your questions.

Can you describe the tree you chose to speak to?

What was voice of the tree like? Was it low or high pitched? Was it a voice of an adult, a child, or a senior? Write down your observations.

Ask your friends about their experiences.

What did the tree share with you?

TASK 10
Speak to a Tree: Adult Guide

Topics to explore:

1. The scientific perspective on how trees communicate
2. Voices of trees
3. Tips for performing the task

1. **The scientific perspective on how trees communicate**

   It has been proven that trees communicate with each other both above and beneath the ground. Scientists believe that trees speak by means of producing electrical signals, hormones, and chemicals, and releasing these into the soil. They can also converse through the scents they release into the air.

   Peter Wohlleben, a German forester, published a sensational book called *The Hidden Life of Trees: What They Feel, How They Communicate*. It has become an international bestseller. The author shares with us that trees are much more intelligent than we thought they were. He believes trees share nutrients and water and use specific networks to speak to each other. They warn each other of harmful bugs and send signals to other trees to protect themselves. The author is sure that trees are social beings and love to communicate.

   A Swiss scientist, Edward Farmer, studied tree communication through electrical signals. He found that in some ways it was similar to animals' nervous systems, which communicates with the help of electrical signals.

   Another scientist, Monica Gagliano from Australia, concluded that some plants can send sounds into the air, inaudible to a human ear, which are received and understood by other plants.

2. **Voices of trees**

   Biologists, naturalists, and ecologists noticed that trees can speak to you regardless of language.

Trees seem to be as alive as people. They are connected to the environment like humans. Many people have experience talking to the trees. They believe different types of trees have different voices. From their experience if you tune in, your mind can hear the different timbres and even identify young or old sounding voices.

3. **Tips for performing the task**

   Speaking to a tree is an experimental activity and is always a lot of fun!

   The first step is to choose the tree to which a child is intuitively attracted. Encourage the child to observe the tree for a while and notice things about this tree which they may not have noticed before.

   The child may start feeling the connection. All of us are part of beautiful nature. We are naturally connected to our environment.

   Finally, let the child talk to a tree as if they would talk to a person, but in their mind. In fact, you are talking to the life force energy of the tree, bypassing a human language.

   You might particularly enjoy communicating with a tree as a family activity.

TASK 11
Share Love with Earth

Dear Readers,

Let us all share our love with our beautiful planet Earth.

Sit comfortably. Make sure your mind is quiet. If you need to breathe deeply for a while, please, do so. It is your heart that will speak now, not your mind. Close your eyes.

Start feeling love in your heart: for your parents, your brother, sister, or pet, and your friends. Feel love for your home, the place you live in. Let your love grow bigger and expand to your city or town, and to your country. Let it grow as big as the whole Earth.

You are here to share your love with our Earth. You can share it with a little bird or a flower, or with a vast wood or an immense ocean. There are no boundaries to your love.

As you send your love to our Mother Earth, you feel it responding to you. Waves of love are coming into your heart from everything and everyone you see. And you feel it all. You sense it in your heart. You breathe out love from your heart and you breathe in love from our Earth. Love is as constant as your breath.

You hear yourself saying, "Sharing Love is the most precious gift in the Universe."

Describe your experience to your friends and family.

TASK 11
Share Love with Earth: Adult Guide

Topics to explore:

1. The scientific perspective on love
2. Ideas for helping us take care of Earth so that it will continue to be a good home for us
3. Expressing our love to Earth

1. The scientific perspective on love

To our knowledge, the energy of love can't be scientifically measured yet. However, all of us know it and can feel it. We can also compare it with the state of "non-love" or neutral state.

The state of love changes the brain's chemicals. It turns on the production of dopamine, which gives a signal to the brain to feel pleasure. The brain sends the signal to the body to create a state of well-being and utmost health.

2. Ideas for helping us take care of Earth so that it will continue to be a good home for us

Our planet Earth is in a very vulnerable state right now. Climate change is becoming a bigger and bigger threat to Earth and to our well-being.

The task Share Love with Earth is one way in which we can help Earth to become a better place for us to live on.

The following ideas can be also discussed in this context:
- Finding ways to eliminate pollution, for example, by using less plastic
- Turning off electrical gadgets, when not in use, to minimize energy consumption
- Planting more trees
- Reducing food waste
- Reusing and recycling

- Walking or biking whenever you can
- Spending time in nature, observing it, and learning to recognize its needs

3. **Expressing our love to Earth**

   In this task we are talking about expressing love in a bigger sense than love between two people or within a family. It is a feeling of gratitude for life and deep appreciation to our planet. Earth supports and nurtures us, gives us a home, feeds us, and loves us back.

   There is an old saying "love heals." Love has a huge effect on our mind. It is not just an emotion. It is a biological process which switches on a healing mechanism not just of the body but also of Earth itself.

   When we breathe, both parts of our breath, in and out, are equally important for ourselves and for the environment. When we consciously share our love with Earth, the planet responds by creating a better environment for all of us to live in.

   Together, we create a profound healing effect and produce a state of thriving.

TASK 12
Plant a Friendship Tree

When Jacov and Lissy asked in Chapter 10, The Tree House Mystery, what could be done to ease the Earth's pollution, Opa Oak replied in vocal Tarrian, "Planting trees, creating wood, brings a happier childhood."

To mark the beginning of their friendship, Lissy and Jakov decided to plant a tree.

They found a pot with a tiny maple tree planted in it in the kabouters' greenhouse. They took it to the meadow beside the treehouse. There they dug a hole in the ground and carefully placed the young tree from the pot into its new home. They put soil around the tree, filling the hole completely.

When the planting was done, they watered the tree. Jakov came up with the idea to put a snag into the ground to mark the place where they had planted. Now they wouldn't miss the spot when they came back to check how the tree was growing. They also put a little wire fence around it to prevent deer and other animals from eating the tasty young branches and leaves.

Dear Readers,

I am sure you would also like to follow Opa Oak's advice and plant a tree beside your home or in your area. Each tree planted on Earth helps ease pollution. Lissy and Jakov planted a tree together because it is so much fun to do with a friend. You can do this too. Then, as your friendship develops, you can observe how your tree grows, while you take care of it together.

Please, follow simple suggestions:
- Research which trees grow best in your area, and what type of soil would be best for it.

- The best time to plant a tree is spring or fall when the soil is wet and cool.
- Choose a pot containing a small tree in the plant nursery and buy or borrow the necessary tools (a shovel, gloves, water or garden hose).
- Dig a planting hole. It should be as deep as the roots of the tree and at least two times wider.
- Put some loose soil at the bottom of the hole to prevent the tree from sinking.
- Put on working gloves and loosen the tree roots. Remove the nursery stake.
- Place the tree carefully in the middle of the hole. Hold it straight while you are filling in the soil around the roots. Make sure the tree is sitting upright and is neither too deep nor too shallow in the soil.
- Build a moat in the soil around the tree, ten inches from the center so that it can hold water.
- Put a stake beside the tree to hold it upright until it is established and can hold by itself. Tie the tree to the stake.
- Fill the moat with water very carefully. Water once a week unless there is rain.
- Have fun planting the tree together with a friend.
- When you finish planting, send love to your friendship tree together. Wish it a good life on your Earth.
- Hug your friend and thank them for their friendship.
- From time to time come to this place and observe how your friendship tree is growing. Notice the changes in your tree as well as in your friendship.

TASK 12
Plant a Friendship Tree: Adult Guide

Topics to explore:

1. Carbon reduction targets
2. Tree planting information
3. The hidden meaning behind planting a friendship tree

1. Carbon reduction targets

Carbon reduction targets may vary in different countries. However, we need to be aware that with the kind of climate change the Earth is currently experiencing, the more trees are planted, the better chance we have to live on a healthy planet. Trees are the lungs of our planet. We need to take personal responsibility for improving the quality of air on Earth along with reducing health problems connected to air pollution and the overheating of our planet. The buildings we live in and the roads leading to them are necessary. However, these absorb a lot of heat which is released at night, warming the areas around. Trees create a natural buffer in the heat exchange and help bring down the carbon levels.

2. Tree planting information

During preparation for tree planting, you may have more questions not covered in the description of the task. Please get in touch with the tree planting organizations or trusts in your area for more detailed information. You might want to know more about which types of trees grow better in your area and are easier for children to take care of. You can always plant in your yard, but if you wanted to plant a tree in a park or other public place, you might need permission to do so. Sometimes planting trees needs to happen in an organized/controlled manner. Your local authorities may know more about it and give you relevant information.

3. The hidden meaning behind planting a friendship tree

By planting a tree together Lissy and Jakov marked the beginning of their friendship. This joint activity has a few hidden lessons within it. First, this activity creates the energy of hope and peace on Earth. Secondly, it brings about a deeper connection of a child with their friend and is a step towards exploring friendship through a fun and meaningful activity. It also allows your child to recognize the beauty of the land they live on and learn to take care of it. Finally, by sending love to a young tree, children send love to themselves and create a compassionate energy space in their life.

TASK 13
Create Live Water

Dear Readers,

The Saashes came up with the idea of creating Live Water in Chapter 13. If you feel adventurous today and would like to join the Saashes in creating your own Live Water, please participate in this process. By doing it, you are helping Earth purify its precious resource as well as learning about another "genius splash."

Take a glass of Water and hold it in your hands. Take a sip and remember the taste. First, close your eyes and concentrate on your breath. With each breath you become calmer.

Imagine standing by the purest creek in the mountains, or by a lake. You know that it is nature's miracle. This Water grants you the utmost life force and energy. You know the Water you are holding in your glass comes from the purest Water source. It is bubbling with the joy and happiness of the Sun as well as the calm and nurturing of the Moon. Feel the Sun pouring its golden light into your Water. Then switch your attention to the silvery shimmering light of the Moon streaming its gentle light into your Water. Imagine the serenity of the woods and peace of the mountains becoming part of your Water as well. Continue holding a glass of Water in your hands and see where your imagination takes you. There are no limits to it.

When you feel that your Water is purified enough, open your eyes. Your Live Water is ready for you to taste. Take a sip and compare the tastes before and after the process.

Describe your experience of creating Live Water. Where did your imagination take you?

What difference did you notice in tastes between regular water and Live Water?

TASK 13
Create Live Water: Adult Guide

Topics to explore:

1. A scientific perspective on the fourth phase of water
2. How to perform the experiment of creating Live Water

1. A scientific perspective on the fourth phase of water

Dr. Gerald Pollack from the University of Washington talks about the fourth phase of water beyond liquid, solid, and vapor. Many scientists say that water is simple, yet some of its qualities are unknown, including its social behavior. Dr. Pollack believes that the unknown phase of water is the top layer of Water, which communicates with the environment. He calls it the EZ layer, or EZ water. You can find this state of water in the clouds, congregated together. You observe it when you put a paper clip on the top of the water, and it does not sink.

It is suggested that Water communicates with the environment with the help of this top layer and responds to the sunlight and as we suggest to our personal "light," also known as our loving thoughts.

2. How to perform the experiment of creating Live Water

A Live Water task is experiential. First, it teaches children to be aware of our precious source for life, Water. Secondly, it gives a child an opportunity to learn to communicate with the Water element. We do it by connecting the light from the environment (the Sun, the Moon, and the purity of nature) and loving thoughts from our being and streaming them into a glass of Water.

Encourage a child to compare the taste of Water before and after the experiment. You will be surprised that you can really tell the difference. This task works well as a family activity.

You can extend this activity by streaming loving thoughts and gratitude into the natural water resources and nature around us. Be mindful that Water is a vital component of everything and everyone. The Water element will respond to our love and light and will share its own with us multifold.

TASK 14
Clean Your Place of Joy

Dear Readers,

Do you remember the Saashes headed action groups of volunteers in Chapter 13 to clean beaches and waters of plastics and other garbage while on Earth? These efforts helped Earth to reduce some of its pollution. The Saashes are Masters of Water. For them it is an immense joy to stay in the water, explore it, and play with it. Water gives the Saashes lots of energy for life and empowers them to co-create with this element.

I am sure that you also have your own place of joy. You are naturally attracted to it because it gives you a feeling of happiness and elevation. You keep going back to it. This place might be close to your home, on the lawn, by the water, surrounded by the trees, or even in the mountains. You can feel its power and all-encompassing love. However, you may have noticed that you occasionally find garbage or plastic, which contaminates the pure energies of joy of the place. This task is for you to join the Saashes and their friends in their efforts to clean Earth.

Think about one of your favorite places close to your home. What makes it your favorite? How do you feel there? We suggest that you go to your place of joy not only to play and enjoy it but also with a mission! You might want to bring along one or more garbage bags, a pair of gloves, and a stick so that you can pick up garbage without touching it with your bare hands. Ask your parent/supervising adult to put a nail into one end of the stick and cut off its cap, so that you can "spear" the garbage to put into the bag.

When you are at your place of joy, observe it for a moment. Look at it from the perspective of a person who has come here with a mission. Evaluate the scope of work. Is the place very polluted with garbage, relatively clean, or quite clean? Does it require much of your effort? Do you need help?

Also, the Saashes and their teams always checked the energies of the place before and after picking up the garbage. Every time, they noticed how much the energies of the place changed after cleaning. To them it felt as if the land itself started breathing deeper and happier, and the air was cleaner after the garbage had been removed. To learn to check the energies of the place like the Saashes, you might want to perform live breathing before and after you finish working. Just merge with your breath, expand, and start noticing.

Note that you will feel a difference in the energies of your place of joy even if you pick up one single piece of garbage which was polluting it.

At the end, after your work is done, send love and gratitude to your place of joy. Now you can enjoy it again.

Describe your place of joy. What makes it joyful for you?

Describe how the energies of your place of joy changed after you cleaned it.

TASK 14

Clean Your Place of Joy: Adult Guide

Topics to explore:

1. Outdoor waste collection risks
2. Learning to feel the change in the energies of the place before and after cleaning

1. **Outdoor waste collection risks**

    Even though collecting outdoor waste is a noble venture, it still can have a few risks which parents or supervising adults need to be aware of. The place of joy for your child can vary from relatively clean and well-kept areas to others containing broken glass, old plastic bottles, highly contaminated sharps, or even toxic waste.

    Please, use your best judgment before letting the child clean their place of joy. It is best to accompany your child in this effort. Your child needs to learn that appropriate equipment, like a sturdy bag, gloves, a stick, or even protective glasses might be necessary to protect themselves.

    Because the generation of waste has increased in modern society, the cleaning is becoming more and more important. It is to everybody's benefit that, along with the cleaning efforts, we need to teach our children to reuse and recycle, to be mindful about garbage, and to be aware of what garbage pollution does to the soil as well as to the energies of the place.

    Please, note that hazardous waste might include corrosive, flammable, toxic, explosive, or sharp objects. Such waste might inflict irritation of eyes and skin, fatigue, trauma, and respiratory issues. Having said that, it is not expected that your children would clean highly contaminated places or suffer from any of these side-effects of waste collection. However, the proper education in this respect will help children understand the effect of contamination on their environment and on themselves.

2. **Learning to feel the change in the energies of the place before and after cleaning**

We are part of our environment. It is no secret that our personal energies are, to some degree, influenced by our environment. By collecting garbage, we not only clean the surface of the land but also remove the energetic imprint of waste from it. Encourage a child to connect to live breathing and through it feel the energies of the place before and after cleaning. This task is experiential. There might be a whole variety of sensations your children experience. The most important thing is to recognize the difference in energies of the place before and after cleaning.

You can also encourage a child to clean their personal space (their room). Decluttering and organizing personal space have a major purifying effect on the mind. A child will feel clearer and more focused on what is important in their life after they have mindfully cleaned and decluttered their room.

TASK 15
Dance in Gratitude

Dear Readers,

Do you remember in Chapter 13, Poseidon ordered Martha to show people's gratitude to those who spent their time and effort to clean the Earth's precious resource, its waters? Let us help Martha in her challenge. I am sure you appreciate having the ability to drink and use clean water every day. Let us show Poseidon our gratitude to people like the Saashes and their teams of volunteers. They spent a lot of time and effort cleaning the waters of Earth. Let us promise that we, too, will do our best to keep our Earth waters clean and pure.

Let us begin our dance. There are no rules, just feel grateful and express it in your dance.

Ask someone to record your dance in Gratitude for your memory.

Tell your friends or parents what you wanted to express in your dance.

TASK 15

Dance in Gratitude: Adult Guide

Topics to explore:

1. The scientific perspective- benefits of free dancing
2. The energy of Gratitude
3. A child's self-expression experience of dancing in Gratitude

1. The scientific perspective- benefits of free dancing

Dancing is a powerful way to make one feel physically, mentally, and emotionally healthy.

It improves the condition of lungs and heart, and increases muscular strength, flexibility, and motor coordination.

It promotes positivity and releases negative thoughts and emotions.

Dancing also develops social skills, increases self-esteem, and promotes confidence.

2. The energy of Gratitude

The energy of Gratitude is very powerful. When we express Gratitude, our brain produces feel-good chemicals, oxytocin, dopamine, and serotonin. They flow into the body and make us feel happy, healthy, and connected. They strengthen the immune system and reduce stress.

Grateful people are more joyful and happy. Gratitude encourages us to notice positive things in our environment. When we are grateful, we open our heart to connecting to the goodness of the world. Moreover, when we express this energy together, we increase the positive frequency of Earth. That makes Earth a better place for everyone to live.

3. A child's self-expression experience of dancing in Gratitude

We tend to express ourselves more often through words. This activity brings out positive self-expression through movement.

This task is a way for your children to observe their own energy of Gratitude through dancing and to learn more about themselves. It is also a creative process. Your children will create self-expression with their body. There are no rules here. Allow your children's imagination to lead them through a dance. Let it bring gratitude, positivity, joy, and happiness to the world from within.

A note: please encourage your children to stretch their muscles a little before they dance. Let them move as fluidly as they can. Hydration is very important! Encourage children to drink plenty of water before, during, and after dancing. Let them rest after dancing and do something non-active.

You might also enjoy joining your child in a dance of Gratitude.

Have fun!

TASK 16
Tell a Joke

Dear Readers,

You know how important a sense of humor is. It makes your friends laugh. It brings happiness and lightens the energy of the room.

I am sure you know a joke or two. Or you can share something funny that happened to you. Please, do it promptly so that Andy and Tommy can get their passes to Zeus's palace, like in Chapter 14.

Tell a joke to your friends. Make sure it is not negative towards or about other people!

Write down a joke or a funny story your friend told you.

Did you notice how the energy of the room changed after a joke? Please, describe what you noticed.

Draw *a funny*, a pass which a clown gave to Andy and Tommy in exchange for Tommy's joke.

TASK 16
Tell a Joke: Adult Guide

Topics to explore:
1. A scientific perspective on humor
2. Humor and social behavior
3. Humor and energy

1. A scientific perspective on humor

You have probably heard the saying "Laughter is the best medicine." It is truly so.

- It triggers the release of endorphins by the brain and makes you feel good and happy.
- It relaxes your muscles for up to forty-five minutes and relieves pain.
- It improves a healthy blood flow and protects the heart.
- It increases immunity because it releases stress and improves the function of the immune cells.
- It strengthens memory. Perceiving information in a humorous way allows you to remember it better.

2. Humor and social behavior

It is known that people are naturally attracted to those who have a sense of humor. Humor makes people feel connected and positive. People with a sense of humor are fun to be around. It is easy to form bonds and relationships through humor. A positive vibe created by a joke unites people and forms a sense of hope and togetherness. By seeking more opportunities for laughter, you strengthen your relationships with people and the world around you. In this sense, humor can be considered an essential life skill.

3. Humor and energy

Humor lightens burdens, heaviness, and stress. It makes one feel lighter and, consequently, changes the energy of the environment into a more positive one.

Humor also brings higher energy levels. It has an energizing effect on the body, mind, and emotions.

Note: It is worth pointing out that sometimes what some people perceive as humorous might be the opposite to others and may even be offensive. In that case, it might cause more heaviness, darkness, and stress.

This task is intended to increase your child's awareness of the multiple benefits of humor and to help them develop their own way of self-expression through humor.

TASK 17
Share a Joyful Experience

Dear Readers,

Do you remember in Chapter 16 how Tommy tricked the god of the underground, Hades, to sit on the chair of Forgetfulness? Consequently, Hades forgot that he was a tyrant. However, he hasn't formed new memories yet. Andy and Tommy need your help urgently!

Please, recall some experience that gave you a lot of joy and happiness. Your help will guide Hades to form his new joyful memories.

The joyful experiences you could share with Hades could include playing with your friends, visiting a nice place, meeting someone you love, or spending time with someone who is fun, playing a sport, a game, or something else. Any memory will do, as long as you felt great and enjoyed it! Please do it as soon as you can!

Ask three people about joyful experience from their life.

Record their answers below.
- **Whom did you ask?**
    1.
    2.
    3.
- **What kind of experiences were shared?**
    1.
    2.
    3.
- **How did it make them feel back then?**
    1.

2.
3.
- **How does remembering it make them feel now?**
    1.
    2.
    3.
- **What was similar about the answers of all the people you asked?**

- **Present your findings to a group of people.**

TASK 17
Share a Joyful Experience: Adult Guide

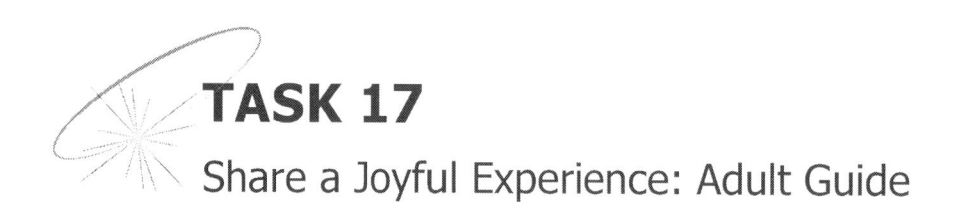

Topics to explore:

1. A scientific perspective on remembering joyful experiences
2. Conducting a simple poll and presenting the results

   1. A scientific perspective on remembering joyful experiences

   A memory is a reactivation of a particular connection between a group of neurons. This connection becomes stronger when we keep reactivating certain memories. When we focus on remembering joyful experiences, we encourage our brain to keep forming feel-good hormones (oxytocin, dopamine, and serotonin). Then they are delivered into the body and make us feel happy and healthy long-term.

   2. Conducting a simple poll and presenting the results

   This task includes basic skills on how to conduct a simple poll. It teaches a child to collect information about a topic from a number of people, to record it, and to analyze the received input.

- Guide a child to think about the goal they want to achieve as a result of this interview.

  In this case, it is to collect memories and feelings about joyful experiences from several people and to determine what is similar in how people feel when they bring back these joyful memories now.

- Encourage a child to create questions.

  We have created questions your child can use as a guide.

- Encourage a child to invite participants.

A child will choose someone they would like to interview. Supervise a child with adults they don't know well.

- Teach a child a few different ways to address adults and children and assist in conducting the interview.

- Guide your child to record responses.

- Help your child analyze the responses.

  Assist in determining the common trend they might notice in responses.

- Participate in your child's presenting the results of their poll to a few people.

TASK 18
Reconcile Relationships

In Chapter 16 of the book, the three brothers, the gods Poseidon, Zeus, and Hades didn't see eye to eye when they quarreled over the division of their territories. Since they didn't have unity between themselves, the three layers of the Earth—the skies, the seas, and the underworld—split into pieces and stopped being united. Earth itself started forgetting about its wholeness.

Likewise, when we sometimes quarrel with our siblings or friends, we stop feeling the unity of the family or friendships. We separate from one another and consequently become unhappy. Even our surroundings may stop being attractive.

In their hearts, each god brother wanted unity. The Tarrian friends were able to show them how to achieve it. They showed the gods that what unites the brothers is more important than what separates them. When the god brothers became aware of this, they not only reconciled their relationships but also observed the unity of the skies, the seas, and the underworld. The Earth itself became a lovelier place to live.

Dear Readers,

This task is for you to use when you are not on good terms with your siblings or friends but, deep in your heart you would like to learn to reconcile with them.
Think about a person you would like to reconcile with.

Close your eyes. Start live breathing. Then drop your attention to the level of your heart and say out loud the person's name. Don't think about what that person did to you or what caused the problem. Just feel how their name resonates in your heart when you pronounce it. Feel the tension it produces.
Keep on observing what is happening in your heart and in your body. Little by little let the tension dissipate. Together with the tension, you might experience some unpleasant emotions coming up to observe. Let them be; keep saying the name until

you feel the unpleasant emotions (like anger, irritation, fear, frustration or something else) have subsided.

Now think about one quality of this person which you like or admire. Anything which comes to your mind will do. Say a complete sentence; for example, "Kathy has a good voice" or "Robert has a great sense of humor." Continue observing how this whole sentence resonates in your heart and in your whole body until you feel completely at peace and in harmony with what you are saying.

Now find another quality you like about this person. It can be something big or small. For example, the next one might be "Kathy is kind to animals" or "Robert is a good baseball player." The most important thing is to keep coming up with more and more qualities and let them resonate with your heart.

When you feel that you can't find any more good qualities about the person, go back to just saying the person's name, for example: "Kathy" or "Robert" and observe whether there is still tension in your heart when you pronounce it. If you feel the tension is gone, you might also notice that any unpleasant emotion you experienced with it is also gone.

Now you are ready for reconciliation. When you see your sibling or a friend again, keep thinking only about their good qualities, nothing else.

We are sure that the opportunity to make up will come naturally. When there is no tension in your heart about the person, their tension will dissipate too. Then it doesn't really matter who will make the first step to reconcile. It will happen by itself at its own time.

When it does, also observe what is happening in your surroundings. Do you start perceiving life around you as brighter and lighter too?

Describe your experience of reconciling a relationship.

TASK 18
Reconcile Relationships: Adult Guide

Topics to explore:

1. The energy wisdom behind the task
2. How to perform the task

1. The energy wisdom behind the task

Any disagreement involves the movement of the emotional energy or "e-in-motion." When we are in an emotional state of discord, we are not in balance. A strong emotion like anger, frustration, resentment, fear, or others shake our whole system, affecting our body, our mind, and our heart. Emotional energy is a wave. It comes, it stays for a while, and then it goes.

When we observe this energy, we let the wave pass through the body without deeper effects on it. When the emotional wave passes, what is on the other side opens up: peace and harmony.

The most important skill to perform this task is to encourage your child go slowly and keep observing what is happening until they feel the wave passing. Conversely, when your child *thinks* too much about what the other person did wrong to them, their mind's energy kicks in and starts creating beliefs, which most of the time, are limiting. Our goal is to keep the mind out of it and concentrate just on the emotional wave passing through the body, opening a space for harmony and balance within us.

2. How to perform the task

Encourage a child to observe and feel the emotional energy in their body. Teach your child patience. The task is experiential. It might take some time to learn to let the emotional energy pass like a wave and open a healing space within you. There is no need to try hard; there is no need to rush. There is no need to be upset if it doesn't happen on the first try. Practice makes it perfect.

The other thing this task teaches is to notice good qualities about people, even about those with whom you disagree. When you encourage your children to notice something good about a person and acknowledge it (in our case, *say* it), they open the space within their hearts for goodness of the world. Then the goodness of the world comes back to us in the form of an unexpected surprise: people around us start noticing our good qualities.

TASK 19
Draw a Dream

Dear Readers,

Do you remember how in Chapter 17, The Shaman's Ritual, Anthony stepped into the drumming beat of the Shaman of Light and started dreaming about his and his friends' future? We encourage you to follow Anthony's example. Dream about your future and then draw your dream! Have a unique and precious experience.

Share your drawing with a friend.

TASK 19

Draw a Dream: Adult Guide

Topics to explore:

1. More about the brain's functions
2. An exploration of the brain's unique abilities through daydreaming

1. More about the brain's functions

Albert Einstein said, "Logic will take you from A to B. Imagination will take you everywhere."

The right brain of a person is intuitive and relates to the left side of the body. The left brain is logical and relates to the right side of the body.

Indeed, we learn languages, analyze, plan, calculate, etc. with the help of the left brain. It is very useful in our daily lives.

The right brain is responsible for intuition, creativity, and imagination. It doesn't care about time. It cares only about a particular moment when we dream, create, or observe. The best ideas for left-brain designed projects, in fact, come from the right brain. The function of the right brain is about a process in a moment of time, while the left brain cares about outcomes. The most important discovery about the right brain is that it is connected to the state of being. It is the state when we feel completely free. There are no boundaries of limitations to our imagination. It is the state in which children daydream.

Research has revealed that, by the age of three or four, the right brain of a child is already developed. The left brain takes longer to develop, and it becomes operational only by ages seven or eight.

The question is, how do children perceive the world before age three? One of the ideas for contemplation is that they are still connected to the Universe and are part of its informational field. Later, children become "grounded" in the energies of Earth by being part of the family and society and by developing the capacities of the logical brain more and more. Before our logical brain develops completely, we are in a state of awareness of the flow of life, which is a dream-like state. This is the activity of the brain, which is not yet measured or completely comprehended by modern science.

2. **An exploration of the brain's unique abilities through daydreaming**
   This task is about exploring the possibilities of the brain through the natural ability of a child to dream. In the book, Anthony was able to access his future, as well as that of his friends by stepping into a wave of the Shaman's drumbeat. He was not thinking or analyzing anything with his left, logical brain. He just stepped into a moment of the dance and got direct access to the information through dreaming.

   On the other hand, Ben and Margo were using the capacities of their right, intuitive brain. As a result, Ben got an idea to create a new type of cider. Margo was guided to resume drawing.

   We encourage you to create a situation for your children like in the story where dancing to the beat of the drum allowed the participants to, temporarily, switch off the "thinking" ability of the brain. Let children dance and dream while dancing. Whatever comes through dreaming is precious and unique. The object of the task is for a child to access the unique capacity of the brain through daydreaming. And equally important, this activity is a lot of fun!

   Afterwards, encourage children to have fun drawing their dream and share.

TASK 20
The Shadow Animals' School
Extra Reading

Dear Readers,

Enjoy another story about your Tarrian friend Anthony, and his shadow bear Duddy!

One afternoon, Anthony and Duddy were walking in Ben and Margo's garden when Duddy spotted something.

"Look, Anthony. Someone is waving to us from the bushes."

A big, mature black badger poked his nose through the lilac bushes. He had an elongated head, a fat body, and short legs. He was looking at Anthony and Duddy with his clever, beady eyes hidden behind a pair of old-fashioned spectacles.

"Come and have some fun with us," he said. "We can use your skills in our class."

The badger changed his form several times, disappearing and appearing again at the same spot. It looked like someone was flicking an invisible switch on and off.

"It's a shadow animal, Duddy," said Anthony in astonishment.

He hadn't realized there were other shadow animals on Earth besides his team's helpers. Anthony and Duddy hurried toward the badger's hiding place.

"Hi, we are Anthony and Duddy, and we are from—"

"I know who you are," said the badger. "I have been following you for a few days now, looking for an appropriate time to show myself. I am Bingo, the International Shadow Animals' School headmaster and teacher."

"International Shadow Animals' School? We had no idea there was such a thing," said Anthony.

"There is one and only one such school on Earth," said Bingo proudly. "When I was released back into nature by my Tarrian master, I decided to begin teaching animals to become shadow animals. They will accompany the children who are ready for them. When one class was thoroughly trained and found their masters, I thought I would teach another class. Soon I started teaching internationally. I'm teaching my sixtieth class now, this time in Canada."

"Why were you released?" asked Anthony, baffled by what he heard.

"Oh, it's a long story. When my master arrived from Tarra, she decided to make her life here on Earth and cut off her roots from Tarra. She thought I would be better off in nature, together with all the other animals. However, I couldn't just lead the life of an ordinary animal. I had extraordinary skills and tremendous expertise. I had to go out and share that with others. That's how I started teaching. There was only one animal in my first class, a caribou. But this year I have twelve shadow animals in the making."

"How do you find masters for the shadow animals here on Earth?" asked Duddy.

"We use modern Earth technology for this process here," said Bingo proudly. "It is called shadow dating. We arrange for a meet-up between the shadow animals and their potential masters based on the criteria they have both entered into our shadow dating system. If the first date goes well, we arrange a few more. Sometimes a couple meet up several times over a year before they decide they are well matched to each other."

"Were there cases of 'love at first sight'?" wondered Anthony, quite amused by this unusual method. He'd heard people use dating systems to find a girlfriend or a boyfriend on Earth, but never to find a shadow animal.

"Sure, we've had a few of those," replied Bingo, shining with pride. "When an eight-year-old Canadian girl, Alisa, saw our incredibly cute shadow bunny, Tsaichik, she immediately asked her parents to adopt him as a pet. Her parents are still not aware that it was Tsaichik who taught Alisa to write her first funny stories about bunnies. Tsaichik supported Alisa's writing genius splash. She grew up to be a famous journalist with the help of Tsaichik's encouragement and lessons in creative writing. When Alisa turned eighteen, Tsaichik chose to stick around a few years longer until Alisa got married and gave birth to a son. While waiting for Alisa's son to become eligible for a shadow animal, Tsaichik upgraded his own skills from writing stories to writing computer programs. Now he is teaching Alisa's son to write software programs in a computer language called Python. That is how Tsaichik helps strengthen a family genius splash. Writing skills in this family will never be lost. They will be passed from generation to generation, progressing and expanding."

"Wow! Wow!" Anthony and Duddy were bubbling over with joy.

"Could we please meet your class?" asked Duddy.

"To tell you the truth, that's why I'm here. I've come to invite you to be guest speakers in my class tomorrow. It is on animal wisdom cards."

Anthony and Duddy accepted this invitation with pleasure. It was agreed that Bingo would come for them the next morning.

At seven o'clock the next day, Bingo knocked on the door of Ben and Margo's house. Anthony and Duddy were ready to go.

On the way to school, Bingo shared with his new friends the challenges of teaching shadow animal classes on Earth. The children were keen to take care of shadow animals, but as pets. The biggest challenge for Earth children was to learn to treat shadow animals as equal partners. Most couples initially went through a rough time adjusting to each other.

According to Bingo, the shadow animals also had their challenges. Even though they were eager to accompany and support humans, it was quite difficult for them to read human's emotions and especially their minds. Also, it was not easy for them to curb their wild animal instincts.

"Remember how Lissy's shadow leopard, Theo, momentarily forgot about his mission and went hunting for a monkey?" Duddy asked. "That happened because he temporarily followed his animal instinct."

After a brisk walk filled with lively conversation, they quickly reached an old barn standing in the middle of a field. There was a nice-looking lawn in front of the barn.

"The class is very excited to see you guys," said Bingo. "Are you ready to share your experience?"

"We look forward to it," answered Anthony for himself and Duddy.

"The bell will ring in a few minutes," said Bingo in a business-like manner.

At eight o'clock sharp, a deafening howl came from the woods beside the barn. In fact, it was so loud Anthony had to cover his ears, which were very sensitive to loud noises.

"What was that?" he asked, taken by surprise.

"It's our howler monkey, Jonny," explained Bingo. "He is our timekeeper. You can hear his voice three miles away. It is absolutely necessary. You see, during lunch breaks our students tend to wander away. Jonny's bell brings them back very fast." Then Bingo added with pride, "He was our loudest candidate for the job."

It looked like Bingo was very good at hiring staff with the right qualifications.

"Okay, time to join the class," said Bingo, leading the way into the barn.

When they entered the classroom, the students were engaged in friendly chatter in anticipation of the start of the class.

"All of our students have already mastered the friendship quality," Bingo said. "It stops the students from following their wild instincts. Our leopard would never attack the wallaby twins. Good morning, class!" said Bingo with authority, bringing everyone's attention to the guest speakers.

The merry chatter turned into respectful silence.

"Good morning, Mr. Principal," answered the class, each in its own language. The elephant trumpeted, the wolf and the leopard growled, the bear grunted, the dove whistled, the cat meowed, and the dog barked. The penguin responded in a loud, vibrating sound, the panda huffed, the chimpanzee laughed, and the twin wallabies coughed.

"We encourage the students to sound their emotions out only at the beginning of the class and at the end," Bingo said to Anthony and Duddy. "Otherwise, the nearby villagers will be worried about what is going on here. Normally, we teach our classes in the telepathic mode."

"What is the telepathic mode?" asked Anthony curiously.

"It's like silent Tarrian. The animals intuitively read each other's minds," replied Bingo.

After the introductions, Anthony told the class about the role of the shadow animals in his mission. The shadow animals made sure the team members had companions and felt safe. They also helped their masters develop their skills, as well as develop solutions to problems they faced. Thanks to the shadow animals' support, their masters were able to achieve genius splashes.

For example, Lissy's leopard, Theo, supported her experiential personality. He was Lissy's playmate, with whom she could try out new experiments with Wind.

Audrey's crane, Lora, was a thoughtful shadow bird. She helped Audrey look at life situations from a higher perspective. She would always say, "Dri, don't spend all of your attention on the smaller details. Always keep the bigger picture firmly in mind." It was due to Lora's wisdom that Audrey was able to prevent the Chernobyl disaster from happening. Lora showed her master the right time to take action before the energy of the situation shifted.

The Saashes' shadow turtle, Martha, was always ready to open her Universal Wallet to the Saashes' inquisitive nature. She was aware that the Saashes needed vast knowledge to be able to learn about the immense potential of their magnificent tri-fold personality.

Andy was lucky to get the funniest shadow animal, Tommy the monkey. Tommy's most brilliant ideas came from joyful activities, like sucking on a lolly. It was Tommy who put a candy on Hades's Chair of Forgetfulness to trap the god into forgetting about his ferocious nature. This required a thorough knowledge of the Greek myths, a good memory, and quick thinking. And it wasn't always fun either. Andy got involved in some very technical and analytical work, which Tommy also had to support, even though it suited him less.

To help the students understand better, Anthony asked Duddy to tell the class about his role in Anthony's life. Duddy shared with the class that even though it seemed like he was an older mentor to Anthony, all he did was support Anthony's thinking abilities. He explained that Anthony himself would always have to make the choices in life.

Duddy said, "Sometimes we make good choices, sometimes not so good. Whatever you choose, you will have to live with the consequences. I don't make choices for Anthony, but I do encourage him to think carefully about the advantages and disadvantages of each option before he makes a choice."

After Anthony and Duddy's presentations, Bingo explained that Earth animals already have wisdom qualities they use on a daily basis. However, shadow animals have to be more knowledgeable about these qualities so they can teach them to their masters.

After the presentation, Bingo led the class outside for the next activity.

The class poured from the barn onto the lawn, merrily chatting in anticipation of a fun game. Outside, they saw that their regular jumping playground had been turned into a class activity zone. There were sticks stuck into the ground all over the place. A round card made of cardboard was attached to each stick. There were two different colors: pink or blue. Bingo explained that these were animal wisdom cards.

"There is an important quality on each card, which a student will have to either show or give an example of. The rest of the class then have to guess what that quality is. If you get a pink card, it means 'show it.' The blue card requires you to give an example of what it means."

"How do we pick the cards?" asked the young wolf named Kekish. He was the most fidgety shadow animal in the group. He always wanted to run, chase, or sniff around. He was meant to serve a master with much energy. Kekish was also the kindest and the most helpful animal in class. If someone had a problem, he would always be the first to help resolve it in a supportive way.

"When I give you a command to 'go free,' you can run around the lawn," Bingo said. "Please don't knock over the cards. You can hop and sniff around, just the way you all love to. However, when I say 'freeze,' you have to stop immediately in the pose in which you were caught by my command. The first one who is not able to hold the pose and collapses will have to pick up the card beside which he or she 'froze.' Any questions?"

A little voice came from the back of the class. It belonged to a quiet, but a very persistent, little cat named Nasty. The cat was not nasty at all, just very focused on smaller details.

"Did I understand it correctly that we have to read the quality written on the card without saying it and then either show it or explain it?"

"That's correct, Nasty," replied Bingo patiently, knowing the better his students understood the instructions, the more fun the game would be. "Shall we start, then?" he suggested, rubbing his tiny paws together in anticipation of fun.

"Will Duddy take part in the activity as well?" asked the elephant, Zumba, the most inclusive animal in class.

"Would you like to, Duddy?" asked Bingo, slightly doubting that he should involve such an important guest in the activity.

"I would be delighted! Thank you for allowing me to participate," replied Duddy happily, remembering how much fun his days at the Tarrian Shadow Animal School had been.

"One, two, three, go free!" Bingo signaled the beginning of the game.

Immediately, the lawn was filled with happily squeaking animals, hopping and running around. The shadow animals enjoyed stretching their paws after sitting in the classroom.

"And freeze!" commanded Bingo.

Everyone froze at his command.

Panda Banda stopped when he was stretching both his legs, one of which was still in the air. There was a pause during which all the animals who found themselves at the most awkward poses had to make an effort to keep themselves from falling. A moment later, Banda collapsed on his tummy, giggling.

Bingo pointed at the panda. "Banda, you have to pick up the card beside you now."

Panda Banda picked up the pink "show it" card and read it to himself. Then he thought for a second of what would be the best way to show the quality written on the card. Then with an "ah!" realization came.

He went back to his stretched pose and smiled broadly. Staying in that awkward pose, he tried to keep his balance as long as he could, then he collapsed on his tummy again, all smiles. Panda Banda had to repeat his stretching and collapsing five more times before the cat, Nasty, guessed, "I think it means that no matter what situation you find yourself in, you need to stay positive. Being positive no matter what happens is the quality we have to teach our masters."

"Correct!" said Bingo, content with the first result, even though it came after six trials. "Time for another round. One, two, three, go free!"

The second round of the game was even merrier as the animals realized it was a really fun activity, like a party game.

"And freeze!" cried out Bingo.

This time the dog, Dog, found himself standing on his back paws with his front paws up in the air.

"I can't, I can't, I can't!" he cried out and lost his balance immediately, falling on his back with a thump.

"You have to pick up the blue card beside you and give us an example," said Bingo, laughing good-naturedly together with everyone else at Dog's clumsiness.

Dog thought for a second and then started explaining, stammering nervously. "Sometimes my master tells me 'You are a bad dog,' but he doesn't really mean it. The point is, I can always tell when the words and the intonation don't match. I will teach my master . . ."

"Honesty!" squeaked the smartest shadow animal in class, chimpanzee Zee.

"Very good, Zee. You are a star!" exclaimed Bingo. "Indeed, you will have to teach your masters to be honest and to always stand by their words. Sometimes it will be difficult because they may not want to hear the truth. Let's move on. One, two, three, and go free!"

Again, the group rolled on the lawn and hopped over the sticks with the cards attached to them.

"Freeze!"

Everyone froze. Zee was hanging off the nearest branch of the lawn tree. Then the thin branch broke under his weight, and he fell to the ground, accompanied by everyone's whistles and laughter.

"Okay, you have to pick up the pink card, which means 'show it,'" reminded Bingo.

Zee selected the nearest pink card and then went around the lawn looking at each card, familiarizing himself with what was written on them. The class was silent, finding it difficult to guess what it meant. Then Zee went around another time, this time poking his nose into other animals' school bags.

"Curiosity!"

"Interest!"

The answers came from all the animals because this time Zee showed it so clearly.

"Yes, yes, your masters will be very curious about many things on Earth," said Bingo. "It is your role, dear students, to support this quality in them. The more your masters learn, the more they will achieve in a whole variety of disciplines on Earth. However, I don't encourage you to teach your masters to show an interest in other people's belongings."

The activity went on and on. The shadow animals learned a lot about the qualities they already had and were to teach their masters. The game was a challenge but so much fun.

The dove, Lova, showed an olive branch. She said this was the symbol of how doves were often depicted in pictures. Because nobody could guess, she had to explain. This example meant the masters must carry the energy of peace throughout everything they do, even if they disagree with someone or something.

The twin wallabies, Tim and Dim, showed how they immediately made up after they fought. They shared afterward that wallabies were the most forgiving animals. They would teach their masters how to forgive.

The wolf, Kekish, and the elephant, Zumba, explained that being part of a social group would be very important for the masters. They themselves were animals who typically traveled in groups. The wolves called their groups *packs*, but the elephants preferred the word *herds*.

In contrast, Anthony's shadow bear, Duddy, and the bear student, Cuddy, explained that bears' strongest quality was independence. Bears were loners, and this natural quality taught them to rely on themselves.

"We will also teach our masters to rely on intuition," said Duddy. "I always tell Anthony, 'Do what feels like the right thing to do.'"

The cat, Nasty, showed the importance of rest. She curled up on the lawn and immediately fell asleep. The snow leopard, Selena, who froze beside Nasty, had to wake her up after ten minutes of waiting. Still a little drowsy from the interrupted sleep, Nasty stated her personal preference was to sleep for sixteen hours. It didn't mean, though, her master had to have the same habit.

"For the body to restore its energy, the masters need good rest," Nasty explained.

Dog was unusually clumsy and couldn't hold his frozen positions. He had to explain two more qualities to teach the masters. The first one was the importance of taking time to play. He said that even if they were tired after running around—or any other physical activity, in the master's case—a little playtime would help revive them, give renewed energy, and support their all-round health. The second quality was the ability to listen.

"Sometimes, it's better to wait and listen, even if you are burning to blurt something out. You may come up with a better idea! After all, we dogs can listen and wait for a long time if needed," he shared from his own life.

The penguin, Pein, was a quiet one. Even though he looked quite clumsy, he could "freeze" better than anyone. However, when his turn came, he landed between three wisdom cards and volunteered to explain all three. He shared that penguins rely on their strong instincts to survive and to breed their chicks.

Pein explained, "We male penguins have to stand in the freezing cold, in the snow, for two months, protecting and warming the eggs. What matters for us during that time is to keep on living. We can teach our masters endurance, the ability to overcome difficulties, and to live in the moment."

"It is time to wind up the class," said Bingo finally after they had returned to the classroom. "The bell will sound at any moment now. I hope you guys and our guests enjoyed our mini party."

Nasty raised her paw and asked in concern, "If it was a mini party, wouldn't our guests get a loot bag?"

"Your attention to detail never stops surprising me, Nasty," replied Bingo, smiling.

Then he took a purple loot bag from his desk and said, "Allow me to thank our guests for participating in our class and for sharing their experiences. I would like to present them with their personal bag of animal wisdom cards."

Everyone stomped, hopped, and squawked—each in their own way to show their gratitude to the guests.

Finally, the bell went off with a loud howl from Jonny, the howler monkey. However, the strange thing was that the howl didn't stop. Jonny continued howling in a voice that sounded more and more like he was in distress.

"We will have to run and see what's going on there," said Bingo with concern. "It's the first time the bell hasn't stopped."

"I'll come with you," volunteered Kekish, the young wolf. He was very good at locating animals who missed class for whatever reason.

Anthony, Duddy, Bingo, and Kekish rushed to the woods. It didn't take them long to track down Jonny, whose thick red fur was noticeable from afar. Jonny was hanging from a tree by his long tail. One of his arms was stuck in a bird house.

"I can't get it out of there. My fist is stuck. It hurts! Help me!" he screamed in horror.

He rolled his eyes in pain, trying to pull his arm out of the bird house, which was swinging from a branch. Jonny's whole body stretched back and forth. He was unable to free himself from the bird house prison.

"Why did you have to put your hand there?" asked Bingo, shaking his head in disapproval.

"I'm a rainforest monkey. I haven't tried the bird eggs in your forest yet. I just wanted to treat myself," Jonny explained, squirming. "Will you help me to free myself?"

"Yes, we will," agreed Bingo.

"But how?" asked Jonny, still trying to pull an egg out of the bird's house.

"You have to let go of the egg," explained Bingo patiently.

"But I don't want to," insisted Jonny. "I haven't tasted it yet."

"Sometimes, no matter how badly you want something, you simply must let it go and move on, Jonny. There's no other way."

"No, no, no!" Jonny howled louder and louder.

Anthony covered his ears. "Lissy would have taught him with her green feathers' trick to stop this tantrum in a jiffy."

"Wouldn't it be fun to build a few bird houses in this forest. We could watch the little birds growing and singings songs. You might love their voices," suggested Kekish.

"I would love to do that!" Immediately, Jonny released the egg and pulled his hand out of the bird house. "I would like to see the little birds hatching, and I would love to hear their voices too."

Soon Bingo, Kekish, Anthony, and Duddy returned to school, happy the incident turned out to be much less serious than they had expected. Bingo told the shadow animals about what had happened and asked the class to figure out which lesson their potential masters (and Jonny) could learn from this experience. The class was supposed to write their answers and bring them to school the next day.

On the way back home, Anthony asked Duddy, "Have you noticed a weird coincidence about Bingo being freed by a Tarrian?"

"I was just thinking about it, Anthony," replied Duddy pensively. "Do you suspect that Verada might be Bingo's former master?"

"Well, we might never know," said Anthony. "And we may not want to ask Verada, as it is a private matter. Perhaps one day she will tell us herself."

Then after a long pause Anthony added, "Unless there are more Tarrians on Earth."

TASK 20
The Shadow Animals' School: Adult Guide

Topics to explore:

1. A joy created from another encounter with your favorite characters
2. Discussing different ways people communicate
3. Some facts about different languages and English
4. Creating greater awareness of animal sounds
5. The computer language Python
6. Communication in a telepathic mode

1. A joy created from another encounter with your favorite characters

It is always sad to part with your favorite characters. Another encounter when you don't expect it brings a lot of joy, triggers a child's imagination, and creates more opportunities for discussion.

2. Discussing different ways people communicate

Communication between people happens in several ways. When words are used to express a message, we call it verbal communication. There are two parts to verbal communication: written and oral.

Nonverbal communication is the use of body language to express a message. For example, we nod our head to show that we agree, saying "yes." We shake our head when we disagree, saying "no." Nonverbal communication may vary from country to country. In Bulgaria, for example, it is just the opposite: nodding means "no" and shaking your head means "yes."

Other common examples of nonverbal communication are tapping, smiling, thumb up or thumb down, varying hand gestures, etc. Because these do not hold consistent meaning across cultures, one should be very careful about using nonverbal communication.

3. Some facts about different languages and English

There are approximately 6,500 languages in the world. Some are very widely spoken while others are unique to a small community or tribe. More than 1,130 million people speak English. It is the most widely spoken language in the world. The next most spoken language is Mandarin.

Languages are divided into families. English belongs to the Indo-European family of languages and the Germanic branch.

English is the official language used by all the pilots on Earth. Sometimes it is called the language of the sky.

4. Creating greater awareness of animal sounds

In this task we draw a child's attention to the sounds various animals make to communicate.

The elephant trumpets, the wolf and the leopard growl, the bear grunts, the dove whistles, the cat meows, and the dog barks. The penguin voices in a loud, vibrating sound, the panda huffs, the chimpanzee laughs, and the wallaby coughs.

Four ways of animal communication can be discussed in this context as well: visual, tactile, auditory, and chemical. The example of visual communication can be that in some species, the males are more colorful than the females in order to attract mates. An example of auditory communication is the sounds animals make. For example, dolphins produce whistling sounds to communicate to others, for example, when they have located a source of food. An example of tactile communication can be of primates who touch each other to show affection. An example of chemical communication might be that of a skunk "spraying" when it feels a threat.

5. The computer language Python

Python is a computer programing language. It is used to create music, games, online programs, etc. It consists of printed commands and codes. Visually, it looks like a mixture of words and characters. It is used to write complicated programs for a wide range of different tasks. For example, Python is used to develop programs for schools and other educational institutions as well as for organizations, such as NASA. In this sense, one could say that Python even went into space.

6. Communication in a telepathic mode

Telepathic communication is a mode of communication between people by transferring thoughts and feelings without either verbal or nonverbal communication. Telepathy is a form of extrasensory perception (ESP). Some people on Earth learn to communicate that way, without spoken, written, or non-verbal signals. We don't know very much yet about how this happens.

However, most people can detect strong feelings coming from another person even without naming it, for example, love or anger.

One of the forms of telepathic communication is remote viewing. A person senses with their mind something remote, without actually seeing it. It is a learned or natural ability which can be developed. In our understanding, remote viewing uses an ability of the mind which, as of yet, is not fully understood by science and, however, cannot be denied.

Silent Tarrian in our book uses a telepathic way of communication, except it is even more complicated. Tarrians are able to convey complex conceptual messages and images and can transfer several thoughts at the same time.

TASK 21
Create Shadow Animals Wisdom Cards

Dear Readers,

Bingo gifted Anthony a bag of fourteen shadow animal wisdom cards. With their help, Anthony will learn more about the qualities that Earth shadow animals teach their masters. I am sure you can come up with even more qualities we can learn from animals. For example, if you have a pet, you might have noticed what it teaches you. If you don't have a pet, you can observe an animal or a bird in the wild or in the zoo and figure it out. You will help Anthony to get extensive knowledge of the Earth animal kingdom. Together you can acquire an Earth element genius splash.

Are you interested in creating a deck of your own shadow animals' wisdom cards? You could play with your friends, the way the shadow animals played in our story.

A group activity. Each person in a group creates one or more shadow animal wisdom cards for the whole group to play with.

Participate in a similar activity the shadow animals played during their class.

TASK 21
Create Animal Wisdom Cards: Adult Guide

Topics to explore:

1. Awareness of the instinctive behaviors of animals
2. The qualities Tarrian shadow animals teach their masters
3. Fourteen qualities which Earth shadow animals can teach their masters
4. Tips on how to play the Shadow Animals Wisdom game

> **1. Awareness of the instinctive behaviors of animals**
>
> Draw a child's attention to the instinctive behaviors of the animals: for example, cats sleep sixteen hours per day, wallabies immediately make up after fighting, bears are loners while wolves are pack animals, dogs are curious, and male penguins take care of the eggs standing in the freezing snow for two months.
>
> You can encourage children to do some research on the instinctive behaviors of other animals.
>
> **2. The qualities Tarrian shadow animals teach their masters**
>
> Duddy, the shadow bear, teaches Anthony about making choices and the consequences of those choices.
>
> Lora, the shadow crane, teaches Audrey to look at a problem (situation) from a higher perspective, to see a bigger picture.
>
> Tommy, the shadow monkey, teaches Andy to study and do thorough research before any venture or project. He also teaches his master to train his memory, to learn quick thinking under pressure, and to use humor to release the stressful energy of pressing situations.
>
> Martha, the shadow turtle, teaches the Sashes to obtain the vast knowledge and wisdom of the Universe, to see beyond Earthly constraints, and to develop global thinking and problem-solving skills.

Theo, the shadow leopard, teaches Lissy to notice, experiment, work with, and learn from the qualities of nature (e.g., Wind).

3. **Fourteen qualities which Earth shadow animals can teach their masters**

   The fourteen qualities mentioned in the task are as follows: positivity, honesty, curiosity, dependability, peacefulness, forgiveness, community, independence, playfulness, restfulness, endurance, perseverance, attentiveness, and presence.

   Encourage children to find more qualities while interacting with their pets as well as animals, birds, or mammals in the nature.

4. **Tips on how to play the Shadow Animals Wisdom game**

   As a group activity, have the children create a deck of fifteen or more cards to play with. The cards are shuffled and distributed among the participants. In our story, there were cards of different colors. The animal who got a pink card had to show or act out the quality (like in the game of charades). The one who got a blue card had to explain the meaning of a particular quality.

   For this activity, your child can create two similar decks of cards: pink and blue. Alternatively, the leader of the game will give the instructions to the participants to either show the quality or to explain its meaning.

TASK 22
Draw a Birdhouse

Dear Readers,

The wolf, Kekish, suggested to Jonny, the howler monkey, that it would be fun to build a few bird houses in the woods. Kekish knew that seeing the little birds hatching and hearing their voices are both miracles of life. He guessed that saying this would distract Jonny's mind from "one track" thinking.

Let us quickly help Jonny and his friends build a new birdhouse. All you have to do is to draw it. Being a shadow animal, Duddy knows how to use magic to turn a drawing of the birdhouse into a real birdhouse.

Draw a birdhouse.

After you and your friend both finish drawing your birdhouses, ask your friend to share his or her drawing with you.

Notice two or three things that you like about your friend's drawing and share your observations with them.

Notice what could be improved and give advice to your friend in a positive constructive way.

TASK 22

Draw a Birdhouse: Adult Guide

Topics to explore:

1. Drawing a birdhouse –the basics of drawing dimensions
2. Providing constructive feedback on someone else's project

> **1. Drawing a birdhouse –the basics of drawing dimensions**
> There are a lot of variations in the design of birdhouses. You can learn more about them in the back of the book.
>
> **2. Providing constructive feedback on someone else's project**
> This task also teaches the children how to express their opinion about someone else's work in a positive way.
>
> When we express our opinion or evaluate someone else's work, we make a judgment. Judgments can be positive or negative.
>
> Teach your child to always start with praising or commenting on the effort a person has made to complete a project. Then comment positively on aspects of their work that you particularly like. When you start your comment with positive energy, you set the tone for the constructive criticism as well.
>
> Encourage a child to express their critical opinion about someone else's drawing in a positive manner.
>
> For example, when you say, "I don't like the entrance to the bird's house. It is too small," you express a negative judgment about someone else's work.
>
> Instead, you can say something like, "I noticed that you drew a small entrance for your bird's house. I think that is good, because it keeps bigger, unwanted birds and squirrels out. On the other hand, if you make it too small it may be

more difficult for the adult birds to get in and out. You might want to make it just a little bit bigger for them."

TASK 23
Learn a Lesson

Dear Readers,

Write a paragraph or a few sentences to describe a lesson you learned from Jonny's experience in Task 20, Extra Reading. It was called The Shadow Animals' School.

TASK 23
Learn a Lesson: Adult Guide

Topics to explore:

1. Learning a life lesson
2. Writing a paragraph, expressing your opinion

1. Learning a life lesson

Throughout our life, we have many experiences; some are positive and some, perhaps, are not so positive. Positive experiences make us happy and fill us with high frequency energy. This is good for the health of our bodies. On the other hand, negative experiences might frustrate us or even make us angry. These are negative, low-frequency energies, which create stagnation, unhappiness, and may negatively affect our good health.

However, if we contemplate our negative experiences and draw lessons from them, the initial unhappiness we have will quickly turn into the positive emotion we feel when we learn something. This avoids developing unhealthy body patterns. We learn a lesson and move on to more experiences with a positive outlook.

This task teaches a child one of life's lessons: to let go of low frequency energies by turning them into higher frequency ones.

Letting go of the behavior, idea, or things which do not serve us anymore is one of the important lessons in life. The natural, healthy flow of life is based on the smooth flow of energy within our bodies, emotions, and thoughts. For example, when we get emotionally stuck in a particular behavior pattern, our energy system stagnates. But when we let go of an old habit, the energy movement in our body, thoughts, and emotions are restored naturally.

The older we become, the more stagnant or addictive patterns we might form. They are much harder to shift because they were formed gradually through many repetitions. It is easier to recognize the unhealthy patterns at an earlier age and to learn to shift them from your energy systems. This will prevent a lot of stagnant patterns later in life and will lead to better health.

2. **Writing a paragraph, expressing your opinion**
Every person has his or her own opinion. It is very useful to learn to express your opinion in an appropriate and constructive manner. This will sometimes be a challenge, but if it is well thought out and supported with strong rationale, it is more likely to be responded to positively.

An example of a paragraph:

I think that Jonny lost sight of what he was supposed to do and instead did what he wanted to do. He was hired as a "bell" by Bingo, principal of the Shadow Animal School. It was Jonny's responsibility to ensure that "sounding the bell" was done when and as intended. After his work was done, he could do what he wanted to do.

The next example expresses quite a different opinion:

I think that it was not Jonny's fault that he got distracted by the desire for the eggs in the bird's house. First, he followed his natural instincts. Jonny is a howler monkey. He is supposed to follow his animal instincts in order to survive. Second, the animal instincts can't be easily controlled.

TASK 24
The Fire Shower

The Shaman of Light agreed to perform the Fire Shower ritual in Chapter 19 for the group. Its purpose was to get rid of unwanted energies by throwing them into the cleansing Fire Shower. All the participants received brilliant new energies in return, as a gift from the Fire Shower. It was delivered in the form of a word, an image, or an object straight into the heart of each member of the group.

Dear Readers,

Would you like to participate in the Shaman of Light magic and get a gift from the Fire Shower?

> The biggest power you have is the power of the Word.
> You can hurt with the Word, and you can kill with it.
> But if you let it go, you will see it burnt.
> It will lose its power, and you will feel complete.

Close your eyes and imagine that you are standing together with a Shaman of Light beside a very beautiful and powerful campfire. You observe its flames flickering in the middle of the night, licking the wood logs. You see them playing together in a dance of transformation. Your Mind understands Fire, it knows what it feels like to be Fire. You see its power, but you are not afraid of it. You respect it. The Mind of Fire respects you back. Fire is ready for you to turn itself into a cleansing Fire Shower. It is made of Fire and Water energies mixed together. They also respect each other, the way you respect Fire and Water. While Fire is ready for you to transform your unwanted energies, Water is willing to share with you its wisdom and to bring you a new beginning.

Think about a word or an image that represents the thought or the emotion you no longer need or want. It can be your biggest fear of the day, an angry thought, or an argument with your best friend. Say the word that describes it and imagine throwing it right into the Fire Shower. Imagine the no-longer-needed energy expressed through that word disappearing into the Fire Shower. Then see or imagine another word, of opposite meaning, or an image of something nice, brilliant, and new, flowing into your hands, through your hands, and into your heart. Your heart grasps this beautiful energy and assimilates it. This new beginning has become your gift. You feel the happy energy of your gift in every cell of your body.

Which word, thought or image did you throw away into the Fire Shower?

What did you get in return?

Discuss your experience with your friend.

TASK 24
The Fire Shower: Adult Guide

Topics to explore:

1. An awareness of positive and negative emotions
2. The energy of a word: negative, positive, or neutral
3. An awareness of Fire's qualities

1. An awareness of positive and negative emotions

The Latin word for emotion is *emotere*, which means energy in motion. Being able to express emotions makes us human. Emotions are polarized, which means that people can feel and express the whole range of emotions, from positive to negative. However, emotional energy itself is neutral. It is the energy of our perception of reality which moves through the body and is felt as sensations. The sensations "color" the emotion as pleasant or unpleasant, positive or negative. When our brain receives lots of negatively or positively "colored" signals, it forms specific pathways for the thoughts, which form our beliefs about the world around us.

2. The energy of a word: negative, positive, or neutral

Our words are also colored by a positive or negative "tint." There are words that clearly express either a positive or a negative emotion, like sadness on one hand and happiness on the other hand. Positively colored words create pleasant sensations in the body. One may feel them as an upward movement or expansion. Negatively colored words bring out unpleasant sensations in the body and create stagnation. One may feel their energy as collapsing or moving downward in the body.

Encourage children to say positive words and to feel how they resonate in their body. They can use words like joy, life, happy, active, loving, etc.

They can also experiment with saying negative words like unhappy, angry, frustrated, worried, or sad.

Encourage your child to feel and observe how the energy of these words move in the body.

Also, there are emotionally neutral words. They are more central and create the energy of balance. Experiment with saying the neutrally colored words like information, harmony, balance, peace, well-being, unique, etc.

The concept of neutrality brings us back to expressing opinions in a nonjudgmental way. We all like positive comments about ourselves and dislike it when people express negativity towards us. While positivity is pleasant, negativity brings out fears and creates resentments, hurt, and dramas. Both ends of the polarity (positive and negative) are, in fact, judgments.

In this task you can teach children the difference between expressing a judgmental opinion versus a nonjudgmental or a neutral opinion.

Examples:

I like the way Kathy dresses. (positive)
I dislike the way she dresses. (negative)
I notice the unique way Kathy dresses. (neutral)

3. **An awareness of Fire's qualities**
   This task explores the Fire element. To understand how we use this element or the way it is expressed in nature is to bring us closer to grasping the deeper meaning and purpose of the elements of nature.

   Some of the uses of Fire which you can discuss are:

   - Heating homes
   - Cooking food
   - Getting rid of the overgrowth of vegetation with a controlled burn
   - Forest fires, brush fires- dangerous, fast, and transformative (eventually a healthy new forest will grow up where the old one burned)
   - Campfire

- Generating heat and light
- Propulsion- for rockets
- Industries- technological processes
- In weapons

The qualities of Fire:

Fast moving, rapidly transformative, creative, destructive, hot, flaming upwards, deadly, consuming, warming, illuminating, etc.

Other concepts connected with the word *Fire* can be discussed as well (optional).

- Digestive fire- the energies that drive the metabolic processes in digestion. You can also discuss the foods that heat the body, for example red meat, spices like cinnamon, pepper, etc. On the contrary the foods that cool the body such as cucumber and mint. Examples of neutral foods are apple, pear, chicken. (The source is Chinese medicine: food energetics.)

- Creative fire- the expression is used to describe generating creative ideas.

TASK 25
Experience a Foreign Word

Dear Readers,

It looks like learning to speak a word or a phrase from a different language can be a lot of fun! Do you remember in Chapter 20 how Lady Mieka and Jakov taught Tarrian friends to say the name of a popular Dutch breakfast? Can you say it five times in a row like you do when you say a tongue twister?

Beschuit met muisjes

Describe your experience.

As a group activity, ask friends who can speak a different language to share other foreign words with you.

Before you ask your friends what the words mean, try to guess what they might mean with your intuition, like a true Tarrian.

Have fun!

TASK 25
Experience a Foreign Word: Adult Guide

Topic to explore:

1. Master a phrase in the Dutch language
2. The benefits of bilingualism in the brain
3. Ice breaker communication skills with a foreign speaker
4. Learning a greeting word, such as *hello*, in a few different languages.

1. Master a phrase in the Dutch language
The Dutch language is not that difficult to master for English-speaking people.

Beschuit met muisjes is pronounced exactly the way it is written, except that some of the sounds are not common to the English language and thus cause some difficulty, typically more so for adults than for children.

It is also fun to encourage children to pronounce this phrase as a tongue twister.

2. The benefits of bilingualism in the brain
It is always commendable when people can speak more than one language. If one starts learning/speaking two languages at an early age, such person may become bilingual with ease, speaking these two languages equally well and fluently.

Learning a second language benefits the brain by opening its hidden resources. People who speak two languages typically develop multitasking abilities more easily. They are usually also better able to sort out relevant from irrelevant information. This ability enables them to focus easier on what is important.

Some researchers believe that people who speak more than one language are less likely to develop Alzheimer's disease. Their brains remain agile as does their ability to remember.

3. **Ice breaker communication skills with a foreign speaker**
   When we visit a different country and meet people of a different nationality, speaking a few words in their language is a nice way to start a conversation and is always much appreciated. This is an example of what are called "ice breakers," something with which to start a conversation and immediately engage others.

   People who develop this skill tend to get to know others quicker and better. It can also provide a smooth way (a bridge) into an intended topic of discussion.

   We encourage you to introduce the children to the concept of icebreaking. What "ice" needs to be broken? People who don't know each other very well tend to be cautious with each other so that conversation may be stilted. They come from different cultural backgrounds, and may not be sure how to approach a conversation, etc. The objective of the icebreaker is to get people talking and working together in a stress-free situation in order to begin building some trust between them. Once some trust has been established, it will be easier to start talking about a more difficult topic.

   Some simple icebreakers are greeting a person in their own language, sharing their names and a bit of information about themselves, asking which country they are from, etc. Many facilitators or discussion leaders ask participants to share something about themselves which no one is likely to know. This seems to work well.

4. **Learning a greeting word, such as *hello*, in a few different languages.**
   Encourage children to learn a greeting word such as *hello* or other simple words in different languages. Once a child masters this, you can encourage them to move on to learning more complicated foreign words.

TASK 26
Make a Snowflake

Dear Readers,

Like Lissy from Chapter 20, you could also give your parents or your friends a snowflake, which contains your good wish to them! You can make your personal snowflake from a piece of white paper, which would be an exact replica of "snow paper." The pattern of this snowflake would be uniquely yours and reflect your personality.

I am sure your parents and friends would be delighted to get such a wonderful gift from you.

Materials: white copy paper and scissors.

1. Prepare a square piece of paper. Fold one corner down and cut off the excess paper.

2. Fold the square diagonally to make a triangle.

3. Fold this triangle in half again to make a smaller triangle.

4. Imagine this triangle in thirds and fold the right third over.

5. Now fold the left third over.

6. Cut the top off at an angle.

7. Shape it.

8. Unfold to show.

Open your snowflake, look at it, and wish something nice to the person you are going to give it to. Give a snowflake with a good wish to your friend, a sibling, or to your parents.

TASK 26
Make a Snowflake: Adult Guide

Topics to explore:

1. Becoming aware of the beauty of the Universe represented by a snowflake
2. The difference between a desire and a wish

1. Becoming aware of the beauty of the Universe represented by a snowflake

A snowflake is a six-sided miracle of nature. It is created from between two and two hundred snow crystals. Snowflakes are unique and don't repeat themselves. They are made of ice crystals formed around dust particles which are present in the atmosphere. When a sufficient number of icy particles have accumulated into snowflakes, and the conditions are right, they start falling to earth as snow.

There are four types of six-sided snowflakes. They create an infinite number of combinations. All of them are unique and beautiful. Scientists have tried to repeat the process of snowflake formation in laboratories but have failed to create snowflakes as perfectly symmetrical as nature creates them. One hexagonal-shaped crystal contains more than 100 million molecules. There are no two snowflakes that are alike.

The physicist Johannes Kepler studied snowflakes for years and published his conclusions in the book *Six Cornered Snowflake*. He believed that everything in this Universe has a higher purpose, including snowflakes.

Anyone who has skied on both natural snow and artificially created snow knows the difference!

We don't yet understand a deeper meaning behind the natural phenomenon of a snowflake. However, we can encourage children to observe snowflakes and to contemplate on the deeper purpose behind them.

2. The difference between a desire and a wish

A desire is a product of our mind. A wish is a product of our heart.

When our mind decides that we are lacking something, we start desiring it. A desire normally targets satisfaction of one's needs and is directed at self.

A wish comes from the heart. It is an expression of hope for other people's success, happiness, and joy. It serves others' well-being and the evolution of consciousness on Earth.

This task is intended to teach the children how to create a positive, high-vibrational energy from the heart and send it to friends and family.

This activity can be extended to making a wish to other people in our life and even to those whom we don't care for very much.

TASK 27
Make a Wish for our Earth

Dear Readers,

Do you remember back in Chapter 20 when Andy presented a flicker of Tarrian Creative Fire in Wish Lanterns and asked every participant of baby Truth birth celebration to make their wishes? Everyone made a big wish, not just for themselves, but for the planets, Tarra and Earth.
I am sure you would also like to join our friends and make a wish for our planet Earth so that it could be a happier place for all of us to live.

Just close your eyes and take a minute to feel in your heart a moment in your life when you felt happy, kind, or joyful. Remember what it felt like and start feeling it.

Now notice that a wish for Earth starts shaping in your heart. It has a similar loving and powerful energy like your memory of happiness. Let it grow even bigger. Your wish is magnificent!

Imagine taking the wish in both hands and putting it inside an imaginary lantern. When you are ready, imagine that the blue flame inside the lantern picks your wish up and holds it within itself. Now, imagine putting your hands around this lantern and releasing it into the skies. Imagine it disappearing high up into the sky, over the mountains, into the seas, or in the woods.

Andy is instructing the crowd to do so just that at this moment. We are sure your wish will come true, and our Earth will be a better place for all of us to live!

Write down your wish for Earth.

Tell a friend about your personal experience of releasing your wish for Earth.

TASK 27
Make a Wish for our Earth: Adult Guide

Topics to explore:

1. A scientific perspective on the human electromagnetic field
2. The electromagnetic nature of thoughts and emotions
3. Tips about making a wish for Earth

1. A scientific perspective on the human electromagnetic field

All human beings, plants, or animals produce electromagnetic waves which resonate with our environment.

To feel this, you can encourage a child to experiment with this idea by rubbing their palms vigorously, and then bringing them closer together. Alternate moving the hands closer together and pulling them away from each other. Feel tension (buzzing) between the two hands. It is an electromagnetic current.

Our nervous system transmits billions of electrical signals in our body with the help of smaller units called neurons. As a result of this activity, an electromagnetic field is created inside and around a person.

2. The electromagnetic nature of thoughts and emotions

Our thoughts and emotions are also electromagnetic. They create repeating patterns in the electromagnetic signals we emit.

Positive thoughts create signals that resonate with nature and the wellbeing of Earth, while negative thoughts disrupt the flow and the natural resonance. It is very important to create a strong positive signal in our nervous system with positive thoughts, which will ensure a lasting resonant effect on the body and life around. Remember, our positive thoughts are very powerful!

However, the strongest electromagnetic signal is created with our hearts. Making a wish for our Earth from our hearts as a group, creates an even more powerful resonance with Earth and raises its vibration (frequency). Feeling kindness, joy, happiness, compassion, friendships, and love in our hearts and making a wish for our Earth will make a huge difference for the wellbeing of all of us. When several people participate in such an activity, the electrical signal we create together is very strong.

3. **Tips about making a wish for Earth**
   You can encourage a group of children to make a joint wish. The electrical signal will be very strong because a number of people will be wishing together. Children will be able to feel it in their hearts and bodies. Because all the children will be wishing the same thing, the electrical signal is focused and will have a powerful transformative energy.

   Alternatively, you can encourage children to come up with a variety of wishes. This will create a diverse resonant field of higher frequencies, which can also be felt in the heart and in the body in an expansive way.

TASK 28
Walk Your Future: Adult Guide

Topics to explore:

1. Awareness of how we usually make choices
2. The method the Tarrian team used to make a choice about going back to Tarra

1. Awareness of how we usually make choices

People make choices every day and all their lives. Some choices are insignificant, like for example, whether to have porridge or pancakes for breakfast. Other choices are bigger: for example, which school to enroll in. Also, there are really big choices, which might affect the direction of life, such as which career to choose.

People make a lot of choices with their logical mind. They evaluate the pros and cons and study the experiences of other people before coming to a decision.

Some choices are made from the heart. For example, a person will know that they will make more money by choosing a career as an economist; however, in their heart they want to be painter or musician. Will they go for what their logical mind tells them or for what their heart prompts?

2. The method the Tarrian team used to make a choice about going back to Tarra

How did the Tarrian team make a choice about how to return to Tarra?

First, the team considered the logic-based opinion presented to them by the Mission Control. Then they chose another method. They listened to their bodies' response and to their hearts' "emotion-free" response. They used a mechanism which is not very often used in our daily lives, which is called the innate knowledge of the cells of the body. This is how the body knows what is best for it. We would say it is an approach which is not based purely on the mind's conclusion or on the heart's feeling, but on a combination of both. In effect, it is a full body calibration regarding what is the best decision.

Encourage the children to listen to their bodies while doing this exercise. This task will help them learn to listen to their body's internal responses while making choices in life.

This may sound difficult to expect of a child. In fact, children find this much easier to do than adults, perhaps because they don't have all the preconceptions and other baggage that we, as adults, have.

In this task, we encourage you to help your child be aware that there are several ways to make a decision. Then in the future, your child will have more tools and will learn to carefully consider all the ways before making important decisions in their lives.

TASK 29
Conquer Your Fear

Dear Readers,

As you know Anthony's friends opened the anti-fear Links in Chapter 23. They helped the young Tarrians overcome a lot of their fears. Do you remember that the Saashes got six lucky days from the Fire Shower? They used them to reward the children who conquered their fears.

Anthony's team came up with the anti-fear template which we are happy to share with you.

If you are afraid of something (for example: darkness, spiders, being alone, having nightmares, not being good enough, or anything at all), here is something you can try:

Try these	Did it help?	Did it not help?
Share your fear with a friend or your parents and ask them to help you face this fear.		
Find something funny about it. Turn it into a joke.		
If you have a fear, do something active to conquer that fear, like riding a bike, swimming, playing a game, etc.		
Say to your fear, "I see you. I am stronger than you." Be patient with yourself. Say it as many times as you need to overcome your fear. You need to believe in yourself.		

Reward yourself for being brave. For example, every time you overcome your fear, give yourself a "brave" sticker or a "brave" candy.		
Observe fear. Perform the Tarrian process, "The other side of fear." Refer to Task 30.		

Which of these options did you find the most useful for yourself to conquer a fear?

TASK 29
Conquer Your Fear: Adult Guide

Topics to explore:

1. A scientific perspective on fear
2. Awareness of what works best for your child to conquer fears

1. A scientific perspective on fear

Have you noticed chills down your spine on a roller coaster or when something suddenly frightens you?

This is a natural response to fear. First, the body goes into freeze and then prepares itself for a fight or flight response. As soon as the signal of fear reaches the mid-brain, it reacts by releasing hormones (cortisol, adrenaline, and glucagon), into the body.

It sets the physiological process in motion. The blood flows to the extremities in order to help you run. Meanwhile, the brain becomes foggy, as the body's resources are all dedicated to supporting the limbs. The heart rate increases. When the stress response passes, a person feels drained and needs some time to recover.

If there is stress from fear in your life for a long time, the body is constantly on alert, which drastically drains the energy meant for life. The body does not thrive; it is living in a mode which depletes personal energy.

2. Awareness of what works best for your child to conquer fears

Our nervous system has a rhythm. Any rhythm can be changed. The frequency of fear can also be changed by an activity which breaks a fearful response of the body. This task offers some activities which help modify the frequency of fear. Trying them out will help children understand what works for them.

TASK 30
The Other Side of Fear

Dear Readers,

Next time you feel fearful, you might want to overcome it the way the Tarrian people learned to do it. It is very simple and effective.

A lot of Tarrians observe the energy of fear by feeling it. They find it in the body and observe it until they see what is on the other side. Because Tarrians know that any fear is just energy, they step into it and wait until it dissipates under their internal observation. Usually when the energy of fear passes, happiness and joy will open on the other side. This process works very well for Tarrians.

Would you like to experience it and decide whether it will work for you?

If yes, next time when you encounter the energy of fear, please follow the recorded process at www.5elementsrejuvenation.com

Listen to the process, The Other Side of Fear, and feel how this low frequency energy is dissipating from your body, emotions, and mind. Instead, start feeling joy and peace settling in.

Share how this process helped you manage your fear with family or friends.

TASK 30

The Other Side of Fear: Adult Guide

Topic to explore:

1. Awareness of the energy of fear and the way to dissolve it by observing it

1. Awareness of the energy of fear and the way to dissolve it by observing it

Fear carries a heavy, low frequency energy. When you are in a room with a fearful person, even the air itself may seem heavy. The energy of fear often hits the stomach or goes to the legs. People might even experience the feeling of being frozen when they are fearful.

In this task we explore the possibilities of the theta brain waves (dream-like healing state of the mind) in order to dissolve the energy of fear. For the best results please follow our recorded process at

www.5elementsrejuvenation.com

Theta brain wave is a "slow" brain activity, from 3.5 to 7.5 Hz. This brain wave occurs during sleep, daydreaming, meditation, prayer, or spiritual practice. It is connected with the intuitive and creative side of our brain and has a profound healing effect on the whole body.

TASK 31
Feel Brave

Dear Readers,

Each of our Tarrian friends has unique qualities. However, all of them share one quality that baby Truth showed them. This special quality is Bravery. This energy helped them save the children of Tarra, and the planet itself from fear dust pollution. You, dear readers, are as unique and special as our Tarrian friends. You have this quality too. Would you like to feel it in your body?

Stand comfortably, close your eyes, breathe deeply and calmly, and relax completely. Now remember a moment in your life when you felt brave. Say out loud to yourself, "I am brave!" Listen to this word resonating inside your body. Feel it spreading inside you, reaching every cell of your body. Bravery is always part of you. Stay with this energy for a while.

Discuss your experience with a friend.

TASK 31
Feel Brave: Adult Guide

Topic to explore:

1. Bravery as a quality and an energy which can be felt

1. **Bravery as a quality and an energy which can be felt**
   There are a few psychological studies on bravery. In most studies, bravery is researched as a quality in the context of displaying it in the workplace.

   In this task we would like to draw children's attention to the fact that bravery is the energy which can be felt and cultivated.

   When a person starts resonating with this energy at an early age, it gives them more tools to venture out with, like being creative and finding ways to identify and fulfill their life purpose.

   Before starting the task, you may want to discuss the situations when people behave bravely. This teaches the children to acknowledge the presence of this quality (energy) in their lives.

   Note: It should be pointed out, however, that on the continuum of bravery, one should be careful not to go too far.

TASK 32

What is Ara?

Ara was the least known element of nature on Tarra. However, during their mission in Chapter 23 Anthony and his team made a breakthrough in understanding this element. All of them became the first Masters of Ara.

Dear Readers,

You too can understand more about this element and take the first steps towards your Mastery.

First, we invite you to collect all the known information from the book about Ara.

Second, we encourage you to form an opinion based on what you know and what you believe Ara is.

Invite a few more children to participate. Divide into two groups. Choose a group leader in each group. Take some time to discuss and come to one opinion within the group of what Ara is.

Each group presents their answer to the question: What is Ara? Each group defends their point of view by giving from three to five reasons why they think so.

Enjoy your discussion!

TASK 32
What is Ara?: Adult Guide

Topic to explore:

1. Presenting your point of view in a discussion
2. Facts about Ara
3. What is Ara?

1. Presenting your point of view in a discussion

The purpose is to present your group's opinion to other groups in a convincing and appealing way. The basic rules for a discussion in a group are simple:

> Choose a group leader
> Collect all the information you already know about Ara
> Listen to everyone's opinion on what everyone thinks or feels about Ara
> Show respect and positivity
> Group leader is to direct the group to a finalized opinion
> Use humor (when appropriate) and good examples

Group leader will report to other groups.

2. Facts about Ara

Ara is one of the five elements on Tarra, along with Water, Fire, Wind, and Tarra.

In the book, Ara is described in the following way:

> Out of all the five elements of nature, Ara was the most complicated and ambiguous. It was harder to experience than the other ones. For instance, it was easy to experience Wind. You could feel it on your skin. You could walk into it or have it behind you. Or you could breathe together with it. You feel it when you move your arms and legs. Fire, Water, and Tarra were also easy to see and to feel.
> Ara, on the contrary, was hidden from direct experience and observation. It was like the primer paint on the wall that you couldn't see but without which the color would not hold. It was like the floor on

which all the other elements walked. Some researchers stated that Ara was the emptiness that allowed the other four elements to be seen and experienced. Others thought it was made of some kind of elusive material. A lot of individuals, as well as institutions, studied Ara. However, their studies had not yet achieved much understanding of it. Because the properties and the purpose of Ara were still largely unknown, many people were afraid of it.

3. **What is Ara?**

Children have a chance to learn more about Ara from the chapter when the Tarrian team were stuck on Ara. Encourage children to discuss Ara as a vital force behind life in the Universe, the Centre of the Universe, and the Creative Force of the Universe. Ara is All and Ara is Love. There can be various opinions on exactly what Ara is. Accept and contemplate them all.

TASK 33
Draw Tarra

Dear Readers,

Have your ever thought about what life on Tarra might look like?

I am sure you would love to have a go and draw it right here!

Draw any Tarrian scene the way you imagine it. It can be Tarra itself, a Tarrian landscape, a Five Elements launching pad, a Tarrian city, the Caves of Wisdom, song, colorful waterfalls, the Fun Memories Entertainment Park, Tarrian firefighters, the Brilliant Way Galaxy, Tarrian friends and their shadow animals, a Tarrian Shadow Animals' School, Tarrians arriving back on Tarra, or anything at all that hasn't been described in the book. Let your imagination guide you and have fun!

TASK 33
Draw Tarra: Adult Guide

Topics to explore:

1. Facts about Tarra to trigger your child's imagination
2. Motivational ideas for drawing
3. Expanding a child's imagination beyond what is in the book

1. Facts about Tarra to trigger your child's imagination

Some key facts about Tarra:

- Tarra is the biggest planet in the Brilliant Way Galaxy.
- It is a creative thinking planet.
- A signal of love from Earth touched the seeds of Tarra's love in the core of the planet. It then sprung back to the surface and gave birth to a whole variety of plants, animals, mountains, and water bodies.
- Having Earth as its faraway ancestor, Tarra is similar in some ways. It has vast woods, deep seas, serene villages, and busy cities. However, even the similar aspects were all different. Everything is bigger in size, less dense, and also brighter. Everything is more colorful, more animated, and more alive.
- Tarra has five elements of nature: Water, Winds, Fire, Tarra, and Ara. These differ slightly from Earth's five elements: Water, Wind, Fire, Metal, and Earth (according to Chinese Medicine and philosophy).
- The most important people on Tarra are the children. They are more mature and skilled than Earth children of the same age. At an early age they learn the art of creation through daydreaming. From this activity all of Tarra's creations stem.
- Tarra's children receive shadow animals as their companions.
- Many of Tarra's children develop a "genius splash" and become a Master of a particular Element.
- People use Tarrian, a Universal Language, for communication.

2. Motivational ideas for drawing

Some of the ideas for drawing can be the colorful music waterfalls forming pink dolphins, sapphire flamingos, silver elephants, aquamarine roses, birds flying in formation, the Fun Memories Entertainment Park, the Caves of Wisdom, the Interstellar Mediums, and so on.

3. **Expanding a child's imagination beyond what is in the book**
   You might want to encourage children's imagination to expand beyond what is described in the book to drawing flowers of Tarra, animals of Tarra, Tarrian homes, etc.

TASK 34

Tarrian Five Elements Radiance Drink

Dear Readers,

Do you remember in Chapter 20 that Anthony and Andy prepared the "Earth Elements Drink," to celebrate the birth of baby Truth? It contained air bubbles, fire sparkles, gaseous spring water, rose quartz, and the scents of meadow flowers. Now imagine what the ingredients for a Tarrian Five Elements Radiance Drink might be.

You can work alone or in groups to have the utmost fun doing it.

Each group shares its recipe with the whole class or a larger group.

The recipe must include the ingredients, the steps to prepare the drink, and the description of its taste.

Ingredients:

Preparation:

Describe the taste of a drink.

Draw a picture of your drink.

TASK 34
Tarrian Five Elements Radiance Drink: Adult Guide

Topics to explore:
1. Imagination of a Tarrian taste
2. Writing a recipe

1. Imagination of a Tarrian taste
Encourage a child's imagination by creating the Tarrian Five Elements Radiance Drink. The taste of a drink should reflect Tarrian's reality and should be unusual to a child's senses of perception.

A hint: Encourage a child to use natural ingredients, which can be obtained by observing Tarrian elements of nature.

2. Writing a recipe
The Tarrian Five Elements Radiance Drink
Ingredients:
- The Zun light – ½ teaspoon
- The essence of morning dew collected from the golden ribbon flower- a spoonful
- Pure Tarrian water – 1 cup
- Wind's gusts – a couple of blows
- Tarra's creative power- 2 pinches
- Ara's love- a pinch

Preparation:
Mix all the ingredients carefully in pure Tarrian water. Make sure that you add the rays of the Zun light at the very end, to provide the best brightness.

Note: Wind gusts create bubbles in the drink.

Taste: Delicious, light, bypasses the stomach, but gives radiance to every cell of the body.

THE FAMILY COMPANION
Further Reading:

Aminda, S. (2019). *My First Esperanto Alphabets Picture Book with English Translations*. MyFirstPictureBook.com.

Baid, A. (2019). *How to Draw: Easy Techniques and Step-By-Step Drawing for Kids*. Rockridge Press.

Briggs, J.R. (2012). *Python for Kids: A Playful Introduction to Programming*. USA: No Starch Press, Inc.

Brule, D. and Robbins, T. (2018). *Just Breathe: Mastering Breathwork.* New York: Enliven Books/Atria Paperback.

Califf, G. (2005). *Making Birdhouses: Easy and Advanced Projects.* New York: Dover Publications, Inc.

Cangeloso, L., MSAOM, LAc. (2021). *Essential Tastes: A Guide to the Five Flavors and Immune Boosting Cookbook.* Qi Journal, Dao Labs and Five Branches University.

Emoto, M. (2011). *The Secret Life of Water.* Simon and Schuster, Inc.

Hanson, R., PhD. (2009). *Buddha's Brain. The Practical Neuroscience of Happiness, Love and Wisdom.* New Harbinger Publications, Inc.

Huber, Cheri (2016). *The Fear Book: Facing Fear Once and for All.* USA: Keep It Simple Books.

Kepler, J. (2014). *The Six-Cornered Snowflake*. Oxford University Press, 1966.

O'Connor, J.C., B.A. (2014). *Esperanto (The Universal language): The Student's Complete Text Book, Containing Full Grammar, Exercises, Conversations, Commercial Letters, and Two Vocabularies.* Left of Brain Books.

Pollack, G. H. (2013). *The Fourth Phase of Water: Beyond Solid, Liquid and Vapor.* USA: Ebner and Sons Publishers.

Reichstein, G. (1998). *Wood becomes Water. Chinese Medicine in Everyday Life.* Kodansha International.

Stephens, R, PhD. (2016). *The Left Brain Speaks, the Right Brain Laughs: A Look at Neuroscience of Innovation & Creativity in Art, Science & Life.* Viva Editions.

Wohlleben, P. (2016). *The Hidden Life of Trees: What They Feel, How They Communicate-Discoveries from a Secret World.* Published in Partnership with David Suzuki Institute.

ABOUT THE AUTHOR

Inna Van Der Velden is a teacher, an acupuncturist, a specialist in Chinese medicine, a healer, a speaker and a writer. She is also a CHILD! She plays pranks on her family, sings songs, and swims with dolphins and stingrays at her holiday home in Florida.

She knows that she will never fully grow up and this is what helped her create your new Tarrian friends—together with the five adventurers Inna shares their inventions, love for nature and even Tommy's humor.

Like the Tarrians' journey through Earth, Inna has also experienced life in six countries—this is what makes Inna observant and loving of all that the Earth's many places have to offer. The nature of her work as a healer allowed her to connect to people from forty-six different countries and hear their stories. Inna, together with the Five Elements of Nature, has helped people heal their hearts, worn-out bodies, and crumpled emotions.

Inna is sure that the art of dreaming shapes the way of life on our planet. It is within our powers to set the conditions for our children to grow up in a happy environment, have more fun, and co-create with our living planet, Earth.

To learn more about Inna, visit:

www.5elementsrejuvenation.com

Manufactured by Amazon.ca
Bolton, ON